How I MOTIVATED MYSELF TO SUCCEED

Top Motivation Tips for
Life, Happiness, Changing Habits
and Resisting Fears

Books by Shelley Wilson

Nonfiction

Motivate Me!
How I Changed My Life in a Year
How I Motivated Myself to Succeed
Meditation for Children

Teen Fiction

Oath Breaker
Oath Keeper
Guardians of the Dead
Guardians of the Sky
Guardians of the Lost Lands

SHELLEY WILSON

How I MOTIVATED MYSELF TO SUCCEED

Top Motivation Tips for Life, Happiness, Changing Habits and Resisting Fears

ZANDER
Livonia, Michigan

Edited by Susan Cunningham
Proofread by Shannon Dolley

Published by BHC Press

Library of Congress Control Number: 2018931005

ISBN: 978-1-947727-47-2 (Softcover)
ISBN: 978-1-948540-27-8 (Ebook)

Visit the publisher:
www.bhcpress.com

YOUR STEPS TO SUCCESS

"Success doesn't just come and find you, You have to go out and get it."

~ Unknown ~

INTRODUCTION

AFTER *How I Changed My Life in a Year* came out—a memoir/ self-help book about *one woman's mission to lose weight, get fit, beat her demons, and find happiness...in twelve easy steps*—I was asked numerous times how I put together the challenges and how I decided which tasks to choose. People were fascinated by the journey I took to complete fifty-two challenges over twelve months, but more importantly, they wanted to know how I kept myself motivated to succeed.

We've all made a New Year's resolution list at some time in our life, haven't we? I know I wrote one every year for decades. The simple task of jotting down the goals I had for the coming year was something I enjoyed doing once December rolled around; however, like many other people, I realised most of my to-do list remained incomplete and unachieved and was typically abandoned before Valentine's Day.

How did I overcome this and manage to achieve not just one but fifty-two unique resolutions? My response is always a bit scatty. I used so many tools to plan, organise, and action the entire year that it became second nature to me. However, I still get asked the question 'How did you motivate yourself to keep going?' a lot, so I decided to collate all the information: all the motivational tools, the organisational and planning schedules, and the personal development tactics I used. It wasn't just about the resolution challenge; it was about everyday life too. To succeed, I had to look at my life as one big picture and then break it up into bite-sized pieces. Not only did I have to plan for the challenge, schedule the blog post content, and physically participate in the tasks, but I also had to make sure my kids were fed, my business kept running, and my sanity, health, and well-being stayed in tip-top shape. It was going to be a busy year, and I needed to ensure that I was up for the challenge—literally!

I spent fifteen years researching various inspirational tools, techniques, and alternative therapies. I read books and articles, watched YouTube videos and took part in numerous webinars in a bid to improve my knowledge, evolve my personal development, and eventually be able to pay it forward by helping others. When your life changes irrevocably overnight, it brings with it a deep sense of realisation that sounds a lot like 'I could have done *this* better'—*this* being life, love, health, or career. I summoned up the courage and strength to walk away from a physically and emotionally abusive marriage, with no idea what the future would, or could, hold for my three children and me. Surviving to see the next day was all I'd thought about for such a long time, and when I was handed that new life, full of possibility, I didn't have the first clue what to do with it.

Turning to holistic health in a bid to begin the healing process—physically, emotionally, and spiritually—was a lifesaver for me. I'm not a hairy armpits, floaty kaftan, and bells on my fingers kind of girl; I love pizza, duvet days, and Harry Potter! So, for me, it wasn't about discovering an entirely new way of life but integrating the personal development techniques I learned into my usual daily routines. Even after everything I discovered, and with all the "hippy" stuff I enjoy doing, it never became the be-all and end-all of my life. The one comment I received over and over after my first book was published centred on me being "a normal person." My three children may disagree with you on what *normal* is by their teenage standards, but I understood what my readers and clients meant. I wanted to find the real me—the one who enjoyed stuffing crystals in her bra to benefit from their vibrational energy and creating colourful mandalas to enhance my meditation as well as dancing around the kitchen to my Prince CD or filling my face with popcorn at the cinema. I was lost and scared, and then I found my inner strength, which set me free. Learning all these techniques helped me to be who I am today, guiding my future choices.

As a Reiki Master Teacher, holistic health practitioner, and tutor, it was always important to me that I explored alternative treatments for myself before recommending them to my clients, friends, or family. How could I advise a lady suffering from anxiety and depression to use meditation if I didn't know about the benefits firsthand? I always walked the walk in my business, and it became hugely successful because of it. It was common sense. You can't fix someone else if you are broken. So before offering a new treatment to my spa clients, I would use the techniques on myself, incorporating them into my life and living with the principles to see if they worked and fit in with who I was and who I wanted to be.

Researching and incorporating so many self-help tools into my life not only helped me on my personal healing journey, but it gave me a grounded base from which to share my findings with others. Only with valid experience and a respectable measure of understanding would I recommend what I'd discovered.

When I wrote *How I Changed My Life in a Year*, I used the many personal development tools that have helped shape my new life. The book you hold in your hand right now is my way of sharing the what, why, and how of making life changes and sticking with them for the long term. I finally understand why my readers needed answers. Writing *How I Changed My Life in a Year* was like making a cake without the recipe. Here was the final twelve-layered chocolate sponge, covered in gooey icing and sprinkles, but with no instructions on what was needed or how to go about making it. Luckily, it tasted great and went down a storm at tea parties, but people wanted more—as is normally the case with chocolate cake!

I'm not a life coach, a specialist guru, or a big name in the world of self-help. I'm a single mum with grey hair and back fat, but I have an insatiable passion for life, and I want to share what I've learned with you in the hope that my journey can tempt, motivate, inspire, and assist you on your voyage of discovery. Empowering women to be the best they can be has become my mission in life.

The decisions we make in life, and the incredible treks we take, don't just happen. We are in control of our destinies, and this means that it's down to us to make them happen. I hope this book fills in the gaps for you. I want it to inspire you to try something new, change a habit, set a few goals, release your limiting beliefs, or stay motivated to achieve the dreams you've already set for yourself. You'll notice that the title reads *How I Motivated Myself to Succeed*; this is intentional. I wanted to share my *personal* thoughts, experiments, successes, and failures, so writing this book in the form of a self-help memoir felt right.

There are a ton of fantastic self-help books on the market today; some even include workbooks that can help you with a specific area of your life, and some are linked to online or audio courses. I'm not reinventing the wheel here; my aim is to give you, the reader, a comfortable read that feels familiar and safe. Self-help, how-to, supportive, counselling driven books are incredibly personal to the individual reader. I've bought loads of motivational books because of media hype or because a favourite author has written it, only to find it to be unhelpful. I slot it on my bookshelf and wait—in time, my life will change direction, or certain circumstances will present themselves, and that book will be just the thing I need to read at that time. I fully support the saying "when the student is ready, the teacher appears."

Don't worry if you feel that my book isn't speaking to you right now; it's not you, it's me! Put it aside and return to it another time, I won't be offended. This is *your* life, and I want you to live it to the fullest. Personal development is a unique journey after all.

However, I hope that you will stick with me and experience a few light bulb moments as you read through the chapters. Our brains have a tendency to store all the information we need but tuck it away in a deep, dark recess. When we don't use these ideas on a daily basis, they can slip deeper into our subconscious. They're still there, but other stuff bubbles to the surface and our brain rationalises all new information as being more important. My aim is to share all the tips and advice in such a way that they become daily habits and elbow their way to the front of your brain again.

If I were going to give you one vital piece of advice, it would be to invest in a notebook; just a cheap one will do. It's a great place to collate any ideas that come to you as you read this book. If you get a smaller one, it will fit snugly in your handbag or briefcase, so you can whip it out and add things to it when you're struck by a bolt of inspiration. Over the years, I've scribbled things down on napkins, till receipts, and even the lining of my handbag—a notebook is a much better option. I'm sure you don't need any motivation to rush out and buy new stationery—or is that just me?

I hope you find *How I Motivated Myself to Succeed* to be your go-to guide when you need a friendly nudge or an unceremoniously large shove in the right direction. Turn over all your fears, leave that self-doubt suitcase at the door, and join me on a motivational marathon. I've tried to make this as fun, upbeat, and informative as I can, and I hope you enjoy reading it and adopting the theories as much as I enjoyed putting it together. In addition to personal experiences, case studies, and exercises for you to try, I've included several lists at the back of the book that you might find useful as your year progresses.

As always, I'd love to hear from you, so please feel free to get in touch with me via Facebook, Twitter, Instagram, my blog, or my website.

Finally, thank you for buying this book and allowing me to be a part of your journey towards a better life.

Shelley x

START AT THE END

BEFORE I introduce you to the joys of setting yourself a goal, planning, and organising your success, or before I reveal some of the incredible stories from the productive women I interviewed for this book, I think it's only right to tell you about the one motivational tool that I find to be the most beneficial.

Reviewing what you've already done and where you've come from is more powerful than you could imagine. It also gives you a great insight into your emotions, thoughts, and desires moving forward. There are quite a few of my favourite self-help authors who actively encourage you to review your past year/half year/month or to perform a closing-down ceremony at the end of a year. Two of my favourites include the queen of conquering your life, Natalie MacNeil, author of *The Conquer Kit*, who believes in setting strong intentions before you begin a task, and Leonie Dawson, who creates the beautiful, colourful, and slightly fluffy *My Shining Year* workbook, which helps thousands of women plan their best year. Whether you are reading this book at the start of a new year or not, a ceremony to get rid of any negative vibes and focus on the positives is always going to set you up for success.

I don't need you to get all hippy on me and prepare a fire circle in the back garden. There will be no need for flowers in your hair, bells on your toes, or a sacrificial offering of two Jaffa Cakes and a bourbon biscuit. A closing-down ceremony can simply be a few notes jotted down in your notebook; no biscuits were harmed in the making of this book! For years I've done this exercise, and so I thought it was worth adding in here in case you've never tried anything like it. You've picked up this book for a reason, and I'm sure it was in the hope of motivating yourself to succeed. The ability to close down all the parts of your life/year that haven't served your greater purpose is a step in the right direction.

It's so easy to do. I'd suggest grabbing a notebook and pen, so you can write whatever pops into your head. All you need to do is focus on answering the following questions—truthfully. Write everything that comes to you, no matter how crazy it might seem. Our minds are incredible tools for squirreling away bits of information that can have a profound impact on us. By doing this exercise, you will be letting go of the past, working out who, or what, can support you and how. Use these questions at the end of a year, month, or week, or whenever feels right for you.

- What did you do last year that you are proud of?
- What made you smile?
- Did you achieve the goals you set for yourself?
- If not, why didn't you?
- What made you sad?
- What areas of your life do you wish you'd worked on?
- What lessons did you learn?

Be honest and open with yourself because only then can your answers help you plan your successful future.

There is one final question you should ask yourself:

- What's your power word of the year?

I love working out my power word for a new year, and I have a small notebook dedicated entirely to my power words where I write everything I can think of that's associated with a particular word. My obsession with power word doodles came about after stumbling across a blog called *Seaweed Kisses*. The author is Michelle, who shares her passion for journaling. She reveals her best journaling tips and offers sneak peeks into her own diaries, while also highlighting daybooks from people across the world. One of her guests was José from Spain, who created a journal so breathtaking that it wouldn't have looked out of place on a Hollywood set (think grail diary from *Indiana Jones and the Last Crusade*, 1989). After seeing this post, I bought a beautiful leather-bound booklet (it's about 17×12 cm) with a tiger's-eye crystal embedded into the cover, and handmade paper. Using a double-page spread, I write my power word and then decorate the pages using my assortment of coloured pens. I write down my thoughts, feelings, and quotes associated with the word I've chosen.

For example, on my "Happiness" page I have a doodle of books (reading makes me euphoric). I've included a list of what brings me happiness, such as my children, my home, my cat, and a few affirmations, including "happiness is letting go of what you think your life is supposed to look like and celebrating it for everything that it is."

You don't have to go to these extremes when a simple Post-it note suffices, but I enjoy spending half an hour creating my power word page at the start of a year. It helps to cement my intentions for what I'm going to achieve.

At the end of this book, I've included a list of fifty-two power words (one for each week of the year) in case you need a prompt or if you fancy creating your own inspirational word book. In short, a power word is just a way of setting your intentions for the project you are planning. It doesn't have to be just one word; you might prefer to work with a quote instead. Write your word in bold letters on a Post-it note, and pin it to a noticeboard above your desk. I also like to log it into my journal, so I see it regularly. As you read this book, you'll get a feel for my obsession with coloured pens and stationery, so you'll understand when I tell you how creative I can get with my word of the year.

It might sound silly to think that one word can help motivate you to achieve success, but it truly can. Stay open to everything that I'm going to share with you. It all works or has for me, but I'll leave it up to you to decide if these techniques fit into your lifestyle. Pick and choose the motivational tools that resonate with you the most.

Think about the power word you would like to use as you begin reading this book; perhaps it's "motivation," "success," or something more unique to you. Make a note of it below, or write it in your journal.

My Power Word:

____

SETTING RESOLUTIONS & GOALS

"Achieving a goal is nothing.
The getting there is everything."
~ Jules Michelet ~

IF YOU haven't read *How I Changed My Life in a Year*, allow me to share a brief introduction. As much as I would love for you to purchase and enjoy that book, you don't need to read it to understand what's going on here. I'll share the back-cover blurb first:

Straight-talking, honest and with touches of humour, Shelley Wilson shares her journey as she sets out to prove that being a fortysomething single mum with back fat and grey hairs isn't the end of life as we know it.

From fighting flab to writing a fifty thousand-word novel in thirty days, Shelley covers a wide variety of themes as she tackles twelve challenges in twelve months.

Now for some opening page highlights:

So much can happen in 365 days, but how many of those days do we squander away?

Take a moment to think about something you've always wanted to do, have, or learn. If you'd started working towards it twelve months ago, it could be yours now.

As yet another year rolled to a close, I decided that if I was going to show my children—and my clients—that it was possible to make your dreams come true, then I'd have to prove it.

Sitting at my parents' house on New Year's Eve, I realised that my string of broken New Year's resolutions would be the best starting point. Regurgitated goals swam around my brain: get fit, read more, lose weight—all respectable objectives until you eat your own body weight in leftover mince pies before the decorations come down! Resolutions abandoned.

I challenged myself to stick fastidiously to completing twelve resolutions, one a month, over the next year. To add to the pressure, I decided to blog the results for the world to see at: www.motivatemenow.co.uk.

When I began the challenge, I had clear objectives: to teach my children that they can achieve their wildest dreams and to show my clients that they are amazing women who can empower themselves to accomplish their own ambitions. I wanted to motivate people with the challenges I set for myself. Never did I expect it to change my life.

It's incredible to think that everything—my blog, best-selling book, becoming a full-time author—started with a simple New Year's resolution list. I'll never doubt my own convictions again, as those initial rumblings of discord allowed me to explore my life with a critical eye.

During my journey of recovery, and self-discovery, I realised one simple thing—*I* was in charge of my life. Having spent far too many years in a dominant and negative environment, I had unconsciously given my power away.

Understanding this helped me drive my future choices. It was up to me if I wanted to go back to college, retrain for an alternative career, and surround myself with like-minded people. It also meant that I was able to influence everything else in my life. *I* was in charge, *I* decided what I wanted, and *I* provided the motivation to follow through.

If I wanted to sign up for an extracurricular activity, then I would sign up. If I thought a choir group, Zumba class, or book club was a good idea, then I'd join it. It's a small, secret ambition of mine to enrol in an amateur dramatic group, but I have one problem—I'm tone-deaf! When I remember this tiny, insignificant fact, I also remember that *I* am in charge of my life. Just because I can't sing doesn't mean I can't be involved in other ways; I could paint the scenery, be a backing dancer (gulp) or be an extra in the crowd scenes.

There is no limit to our goals and dreams if we only allow ourselves the opportunity to believe that they're possible. Remember—by being in charge of your life, you give yourself permission to succeed.

A QUICK NOTE ABOUT LIST WRITING

In this chapter, I want to talk about the goals I set for myself and hopefully, help you to think through your ambitions for the future. We could all whip out a notepad on 1 January and write the usual nonsense. My archaic New Year's resolution list looked something like this:

- Write a book
- Read more
- Lose weight
- Do the ironing
- Go out with friends regularly

It waffled on and on, but you get the idea—it was the same year after year, and on reflection, I was setting myself up to fail with every resolution list I wrote.

First of all, I was never going to get to the bottom of the ironing pile because this is one household job I despise. In fact, my ironing pile is so high that I spotted a mountain goat teetering near the top last week. "Write a book" always got the top spot because it's been a dream of mine since I was eight years old. Reading and reviewing is something I adore, so this was a cheat resolution because I knew that I'd get through about fifty books over the course of a year and be able to tick at least one item off my list.

If I truly wanted to succeed, I would have to use an alternative tactic. Why? Because the old way wasn't working. I realised, when faced with a task or a problem, I invariably pigeonholed it into a familiar setting. I'd got far too comfortable at failing. As I looked at yet another New Year's resolution list, I understood that I was following the same path but expecting different results. It was quite an uplifting revelation. My addiction to list writing meant that this was my default setting for anything and everything I wanted to complete. Willpower had nothing to do with it!

If my deeply ingrained list-writing habit was a hindrance rather than a help, then I knew I had to re-evaluate my actions. I decided to use my list as a guideline for the next part of my challenge. It was the blueprint on which to base all the changes I needed to make to succeed. The list was just the beginning. I discovered that working out *what* to write down was a much more important task.

What does your resolution list look like? Do you notice a similar pattern? Don't panic—it is possible to choose goals/tasks/resolutions, whatever you want to call them, which are so meaningful that you look forward to working on them.

The final list that ended up being the basis for *How I Changed My Life in a Year* covered something from every area of my life. It might look immense when you see it in list form, but I'll get to how I broke down each section later.

- Lose weight
- Get fit
- Do something creative
- Give up the demon drink
- Do something I've never done before
- Adopt better habits
- Appreciate what I have by giving something up
- Get out and about more
- Learn something new
- Be happy and grateful
- Conquer my fears
- Make homemade gifts

The media is flooded with articles on goal setting, resolutions, and weight-loss regimes at the start of a new year. There are plenty of challenges available for us to take part in, but is it right to sign up for the first experience we come across? No, this would be disastrous for our development and our soul. Working out what we want to achieve takes time and thought.

You may rush to add a trek to Machu Picchu to your to-do list. This is a noble goal and one that I have on my bucket list. Deciding to travel across the world and climb to the top of a mountain isn't something that many of us can just do. It takes planning and funding—all of which take time.

As a single mum of three, I know that taking a trip to Peru is a long-term goal—something for when my children are self-sufficient and can cope without me for a longer period. At the moment, I can't even take a bath without them camping outside the bathroom door demanding to know why the Wi-Fi isn't working, if there's anything to eat, or if I have any money in my purse for a school trip.

When I finally settled on the twelve topics for my challenge list, I was pleased with the outcome. It had taken some weeks for me to decide on the areas of my life that I wanted to change. Don't get me wrong; my life is pretty great. I'm healthy(ish) and happy(ish), but there's always room for improvement. Do you ever feel like something is missing? That's what it was like for me. I loved running my business, my kids were in a great place emotionally and did well at school, I had loads of friends and a supportive family, but there was a void that I needed to fill—I just didn't know what it was.

Eventually, I recognised that for many years I'd drifted through life. Work, play, sleep, eat, and repeat. There was nothing exceptional about me or my life. I had no great aspirations beyond paying the bills and filling the fridge. That was the wake-up call I needed to turn everything around. I'm sure you must be thinking, but why bother? How could writing a to-do list help change your life?

WHY BOTHER?

Think back on all the sporting events that you've watched over the years: the Olympics, Paralympics, Rugby World Cup, Tour de France, Super Bowl, or Wimbledon. What do they all have in common? The answer is top-level athletes. These guys set themselves a goal and give 100 percent to achieve it. The majority will have personal coaches who work with them to focus their mind, train their bodies towards a specific deadline, and manage their time effectively. This is personal development at its best. They have a clear outline of what is needed to succeed.

Setting a goal gives you a starting point; it helps you to think about yourself for a change, and it's the ideal process to visualise a better future.

Deciding on what goals you want to set will be personal to you. Your interests may include abseiling, calligraphy, running a marathon, teaching adult learners, launching a new career/business, or any number of incredible opportunities. Writing down all the possibilities is a great place to start; it allows your brain to open up to new ideas and work through outdated ones. Once you start writing, your subconscious mind will kick in and dig deep for all the hidden gems, long-forgotten dreams, and ideas that you might have been playing around with but never nailed down. I can't tell you what to add to your list, but I can show you how I chose the right things for me, and hopefully it will unlock something in you.

WHAT DO YOU WANT?

Corporate businesses help their workforce decide on weekly/monthly/yearly outcomes by adopting the SMART goal-setting acronym. I've even heard one of my son's teachers use it to help him revise for an exam. SMART stands for

Specific: You know exactly what you want to achieve.

Measurable: You know the targets and milestones to track your progress.

Achievable: Your goal can be achieved.

Realistic: Your goal fits in with your life/business needs.

Timely: You have a deadline to achieve your goal.

"A goal without a plan is just a wish."

~ Antoine de Saint-Exupery ~

It's a winning formula for setting goals and is used worldwide. Can we adopt the same principles for our lifestyle aims? Yes, of course we can—once we know *what* we want to achieve.

Think about your reasons for choosing this book. Was it the attractive cover? The inspirational blurb? Or perhaps you read the title and thought "I need a bit of motivation to succeed in my life." As you toyed with the choice of buying, what thoughts were going through your head? Did you have a specific theme or idea that pushed its way to the forefront of your mind? Write it down in your notebook. Identifying what you are passionate about is the ideal place to start.

When I think about my needs, I tend to lean towards creativity. Yes, I do want to lose weight and maintain my fitness, and I'd also love to be able to speak Italian. However, my writing goals take over my every waking moment. Plotting out my young adult fantasy novels, writing my personal development courses, and preparing content for my blogs are my most important objectives.

What are your aspirations? What do you think about most often? It will fill your thoughts morning, noon, and night. Grab your notebook and jot down anything that springs to mind. Maybe you are always thinking about food and your health. What about training in nutrition and helping others to improve their well-being? Perhaps there's a vacant store in your area, and you dream of opening a coffee/book/jewellery shop. Do you have a young family and long to work for yourself, from home, so that you can be close to them? Finding your passion will drive your determination and influence your success.

However, you won't be able to define what "success" is to you without adopting the SMART acronym. One of the challenges I set for myself was to conquer my fears. This may sound like an impossibility, especially if you spend a few moments thinking about your own fears—I know I could probably fill an entire notebook on this topic alone. Instead of feeling overwhelmed by such a vague goal, I made this particular challenge specific to one area of my life and adopted the SMART system.

Here's how it came out:

Goal = Conquer my fears

For many years, I longed to take part in NaNoWriMo (National Novel Writing Month) but dropped out at the last minute for fear of failure. The contest takes place every November, so I added this to my resolution challenge for that month. Once it made the list, I became accountable for my actions—there was *no* turning back.

Specific: Write a fifty thousand-word novel.

Measurable: Write 1,666 words a day for thirty days.

Achievable: Over four hundred thousand writers take part in the contest every year.

Realistic: I want to be a published author; this brings me a step closer.

Timely: The deadline is midnight on 30 November.

I took part in my first NaNoWriMo event in 2013 and attained my "winner" status (an online sticker to add to your blog/website) nine days into the contest. In 2014, I took part again and reached the fifty thousand-word mark by the end of the second week. I returned once more the following year and completed my manuscript within the allotted time. I have taken part consistently since I first started and hope to continue to write during NaNoWriMo for many years to come. Taking part in this venture has cemented my "*I* am in control" mentality. My family and friends know how important this is to me and joke about me bolting the doors and switching off my phone. I laugh and tell them I'll see them in December for a catch-up.

I'm passionate about my writing; I'm dedicated to achieving this goal, and I therefore plan my time accordingly, so I can stay motivated and achieve that "winner" status.

One of my favourite sayings that I have displayed on my noticeboard and which challenges my goal-setting techniques whenever I read it is "Behind every no entry sign there is a door." It's so simple and yet powerful at the same time. When I originally wrote my goal, "write a book," it lacked some passion and drive. That "write a book" was the no entry sign; how on earth was I going to achieve that and create something from nothing? When I changed it slightly to "I will write the first draft of my young adult fantasy novel by the end of November," it became a door that I knew could be opened if I dedicated my time and energy to it. Look over your own resolution/goals list, and see where you can add "I will..." and turn that no entry sign into a door. If you need to go one step further, try adding "I am..." and smash that door off its hinges. Suddenly, your goal becomes a reality.

There are so many goals you can set for yourself; the world is your oyster, and in this book, I'm sharing a mix of the challenges I set for myself, but these tasks don't have to be huge or life changing. Goals can be simple acts that you want to introduce into your family life, such as eating dinner together four nights a week. Don't worry if your desires aren't big, life-altering statements. Since completing my resolution challenge a couple of years ago, my goals have been much calmer and included the following:

- Eat vegetables at every evening meal.
- Meet someone I admire every week for a quick coffee.
- Learn how to add a WordPress plug-in to my blog.
- Meditate every day for ten minutes.
- Read a chapter a day of a fiction novel.

Don't get hung up on the "what." Devote your time and energy to making them happen and achieving success.

VISUAL TOOLS TO HELP YOU FIGURE OUT WHAT YOU WANT TO ACHIEVE

I'm a visual learner, which means I love making mind maps, charts, doodling on notepads, and creating vision boards. The mind map is a marvellous personal development technique to use if you're struggling to think about what you want to achieve. Grab your notebook, and let's have a go. It's such a simple exercise and can reward you with more ideas than you know what to do with.

Use seven or eight pages in your notebook, and draw a small circle in the middle of each page. In each circle, write one of the following headings (or choose your own titles):

- Career/Business/Job
- Finances
- Family/Friends/Relationships
- Creativity
- Physical/Mental health
- Leisure activities
- Personal development

Using coloured pens (I like to get carried away with my mind maps—the more colourful the better), write as many words/phrases as possible that you associate with the page heading. Don't think too hard about it; just write down what comes to you.

For example, when I was working on my resolution/goals list, I knew that "writing" needed to play a vital role in the entire process, so instead of using "creativity" as a heading, I used "writing." My mind map for that goal looked like this:

Goal = Writing

- Take part in National Novel Writing Month.
- Start a blog.
- Enter one short story competition a month.
- Use my journal daily.
- Be approached by a publisher/agent.
- Join Twitter and engage with the writing community.
- Read how-to books and improve my writing skills.
- Keep a story idea diary in my bag.
- Finish the first draft of a young adult novel.

Repeat this exercise for all the key areas in your life and see what comes up. If you find that one of the subject headings has more words or phrases on the page, take a look at what you've written and see if a goal jumps out at you. For the record, I achieved everything on my mind map apart from entering one short story competition a month.

Here's another example: your "physical/mental health" page might be full of healthy recipe ideas or a range of alternative fitness classes that you fancy trying out. You could write about your interest in health and well-being from the perspective of becoming a personal trainer or counsellor.

The best advice I can give you when doing this exercise is not to hold back. Don't think too hard about it; just write anything that comes to mind—however crazy it might seem. Dream big, think bigger. If you want to include on your "leisure/activities" page that you would love to meet Benedict Cumberbatch, then add it. Who knows what might happen in the future? You might become a theatre reviewer, join a drama club or write a blog and find yourself face-to-face with the man himself. Remember the saying, "*I* am in control of my life."

If you're interested in seeing some of the mind maps I've created, pop over to my Pinterest account and look at the *How I Motivated Myself to Succeed* board. I've added quite a few pins that might be useful to you, whether I've spoken about them in this book, or I spotted them on the go. www.pinterest.com/MotivateMeBlog

By using the mind map technique, I was able to determine the areas of my life that I wanted to work on the most. Health, fitness, creativity, my environment, and leisure activities all provided a host of words and phrases that left me feeling excited about the prospect of including them on my yearlong challenge. I came away with such a variety of ideas about what I would like to include. The maps were incredibly useful. However, there was another tool that I used in conjunction with them, which gave me another visual target—vision boards.

I adore making vision boards. I run personal development workshops on this topic and spend a few hours every New Year's Day creating a new board for the coming year. As a visual learner, I find this tool to be a powerful addition to my self-care toolbox.

If you've never heard about vision boards before, allow me to fill you in. A vision board is similar to a collage. It's a visual representation of all the things you want to be, do, and have in your life. I've written a beginner's guide on the topic as part of my Wellbeing Workshop series, which is available at all major retailers.

I wrote this guide to complement my courses, but the little handbag-sized guide has proved to be quite popular. Interestingly, one book reviewer made the valid point that there is a lack of images in the book—something I hadn't considered on publication—so if you do want to see some examples, pop over to my vision board section on Pinterest: www.pinterest.com/MotivateMeBlog.

When I run my courses, I give my students a handout with a series of thought-provoking questions. I've included a couple of the questions here for you. Take a quick look at them and make a note of your answers in your journal—they might come in handy when you're goal setting.

- List your top five achievements/memories/successes.
- List five things you want the most.
- If you had five other lives to lead, what would you do?
- Write five experiences you would like to enjoy (e.g. taking a hot-air balloon trip).

I always find that this exercise gets the subconscious juices flowing and allows you to dream big and be free to imagine yourself doing, having, or being anything at all.

Here are a few examples from the list I wrote when I did this exercise:

> Achievements/memories/successes: Having my three kids when I was told that I wouldn't be able to have children, going on a solo holiday, opening my holistic health business, publishing a book and hitting the bestseller list
>
> What I want: To be a size twelve, to own a VW camper van, to have a popular blog
>
> Lives I'd lead: Parapsychologist, forensic scientist, vampire slayer, author
>
> Experiences: Trek to Machu Picchu, meet my favourite author (I've ticked this off my list), visit a film set while Johnny Depp is filming

I realise I might never get to meet Mr. Depp or be the next vampire slayer, but I do write fantasy fiction for young adults, and so there's every possibility that I will be able to channel my inner Buffy into one of my stories. Visualising your dreams, however wacky, helps you to unlock your deepest desires and appreciate all your achievements.

Glance over your triumphs and harness those feelings of pride, happiness, and determination. Begin to focus on the kind of goals you can work on that will replicate the motivation you felt when you experienced them.

If you want to have a go at making your own vision board straightaway, it's very simple. Grab a cheap corkboard or a large piece of strong cardboard, some scissors, a pen, glue, and an assortment of magazines (try to pick ones that you wouldn't normally read). Once you have your equipment, you can start to flick through the magazines. If you know that over the coming year you will be changing your job, then look for photographs, wording, and pictures that represent the new role you are interested in. If you plan to start a family, look for cute baby pictures and photographs of pregnant women. If you want to move to a new house, then find pictures that represent the area you want to live in (by the sea/in the city) and the type of property you want.

If, like me, you sometimes haven't a clue what you want, just flick through the magazines and cut out any words, pictures, and photographs that catch your eye and make you smile. You may have no idea what direction your board is going—don't worry, this is normal and once you start to stick the pictures down a pattern will begin to emerge. I've created loads of boards with little to no aspirations, and yet as I add pictures a common theme will begin to form. I was quite ill a few years ago and ended up having to close my holistic business and rethink my entire life. I created a vision board to help me work out which direction to take. Fortunately, I had my writing and book sales to help me pay the bills, so I thought that my work, although now going in a different direction, was going to be the main focus. I went looking for photographs of books and stationery, but when I stepped back and took a closer look, I noticed that health and well-being images had taken over my board and my theme was "all about you." It became evident fairly quickly that I needed to concentrate on my body and mind. Remember: you can't fix others if you are broken.

Vision boards are such a wonderful personal development tool, and you can redo them whenever you want or add to your board over the week/month/year. It's also a great exercise to do with the family. Children love the cut and stick projects, and it can be quite eye-opening as a parent to see the ambitions your child has and the dreams they want to fulfil either over the coming year or as part of their future. Make it a family activity on New Year's Day and celebrate each other's creations.

Once you're happy with your board, put it up where you can see it every day. Keep looking at it and imagine yourself living the life that your board reflects.

"Dream it, live it, become it."

You can use vision boards as part of your planning or organising techniques, or you can use them as motivation to complete your goals. I have one wall in my office where I hang all of my favourite boards. It's like stepping into another world, full of opportunities, exciting trips, and ambitions, when I glance at that wall. It also keeps me focused on my ultimate goals and helps me to remain driven when planning and writing my blog content and books.

Focus not only on the pictures you've chosen but also on the process. You might have a board covered in images of a red Ferrari and wads of cash (the "want"), but these are just the results you are hoping for. Concentrating on making money and getting a job at a Ferrari dealership is how you produce the results (the process).

Your vision board will not miraculously deliver everything your heart desires. If this were the case, I would be celebrating my tenth wedding anniversary with Johnny Depp around now. Vision boards are our inspiration and our motivation to achieve our wildest dreams.

We see the images of everything we want in life displayed in a prominent position in our home. We see it, we think about it, we take action steps to make it happen. This, in turn, manifests the real thing.

"Thoughts become things. If you see it in your mind, you will hold it in your hand."

~ Bob Proctor ~

It's important to note that if we don't truly believe 100 percent in our goals and desires, then they won't happen. I joke about my obsession with Johnny Depp, and his photo has made it onto some of my boards over the years. However, I am under no illusion that he will knock on my door. His picture makes me smile, but I know deep down that I won't walk past him in Tesco anytime soon. The picture of a cute puppy, however, is something I can manifest when the time is right... and I can always call it Captain Jack!

Now is probably the perfect time to tell you: there is no obligation for you to embark on a twelve-month motivational slog in a bid to change your life. You might only want to work on one particular goal, or just try to mix it up a bit in the daily grind. Perhaps you bought this book looking for a little inspiration and a pick-me-up to keep you focused on a project you're already doing. Of course, if you are in favour of the longer challenge, then go for it! I can highly recommend it, but don't stress about it. Starting my blog began as a bit of fun; it was my dedication and passion that turned it into a full-time career.

BREAKING DOWN YOUR GOALS

You might have noticed that my resolution list has twelve items on it, but the description of *How I Changed My Life in a Year* mentions fifty-two challenges. There is a sound reason for this discrepancy.

When I began blogging about this challenge on 1 January 2013, I wrote my first post introducing myself and what I hoped to achieve over the coming year and then detailed the twelve items on my list. It only dawned on me *after* I hit publish that there may be some blogger etiquette that I should follow. I'd never done anything like this before and had to learn as I went along. Therefore, to ensure that I was blogging correctly, I researched tons of other blogs from a variety of genres to see the kinds of articles they posted, the images they used, and the types of audiences they attracted. It was only at this point that I noticed how regularly bloggers published their content. Weekly posts appeared in their feeds, and each article was as engaging as the previous one. I wasn't prepared for that.

Using the mind map method once again, I wrote each challenge on a page and did a brainstorming session to see what things I could come up with. It was an incredibly useful exercise and allowed me to break every goal into sections.

As I was taking part in monthly goals, I broke them into four parts, so I could do a new post every week. For my "Get Fit" month, I extracted four exercises from my mind map and used these as the basis for my challenge, like this:

Month Two = Get Fit

Week 1: Skipping

Week 2: Walking

Week 3: Wii Fit

Week 4: Cycling

It worked well, not just for the blog but also for my sanity. I now had a smaller, more specific goal, which was measurable, achievable, realistic and timely (SMART). The fact that I'd set myself up for such a huge undertaking was no longer overwhelming because I could handle it one week at a time.

One of the questions I have been asked numerous times by my readers is whether I was strict with my themes. They want to know if I was only concentrating on that specific topic in that week/month, or if I carried them on. The truth is, I carried some of them on when it was appropriate. Month one, for example, was all about weight loss, and by the end of January, I'd lost a total of ten pounds. I hadn't achieved my original goal of wanting to lose a stone in weight, so I stuck with the principles I'd put in place during that first month and applied them alongside the new theme, "Get Fit," in month two. Once I'd achieved my weight loss, I could tick it off the list; although, for me, body image and fitness are ongoing battles that require careful maintenance on my part and take up a fair amount of my life. It's quite nice when two goals overlap and complement each other in such a way, especially when one of the phrases I'd jotted on my mind map was "eat less, move more!"

Breaking down a bigger goal is a great way of achieving success. Hopefully, you'll have some idea of what you want to change, do, or have. Top Tip: these are *your* goals, not your husband's/wife's/kids'/parents'/bosses' goals; you need to own them.

Let's look at another example of how to break a big goal into smaller, more manageable pieces.

Goal = Write a book

If you have no other idea beyond a passionate need to write a book, mind map this topic on a sheet of paper and include anything that comes to you. It might be things like this:

- e-book/Paperback
- **Fiction**
- Character biographies/names
- Settings
- Length of novel/novella

- Market/Audience
- **Nonfiction**
- Topic/Theme
- Length of book
- Research needed
- **Publishing**
- Beta readers
- Editor
- Cover designer
- Marketing/Promotion

Let's assume you decide to write a nonfiction book about growing potatoes (it's possible). You can prepare a second mind map that is slightly more relevant. This time you would record everything you need to include in your spud book.

Goal = Write and publish my *Potatoes for Life* book.

- Publish as e-book and paperback
- Ten chapters
- The history of the potato
- Preparing the ground for planting your potato
- Potato recipe ideas

You get the picture.
Now apply the SMART acronym to your idea.

Specific: Write an eighty thousand-word book called *Potatoes for Life*.

Measurable: Write eight hundred words a day, five days a week for five months to achieve the first draft.

Achievable: Allocate two hours every morning/night to my writing.

Realistic: I have won "allotment of the year" for my prize potatoes for three years in a row and "biggest spud" award at the horticultural show.

Timely: Arrange a read-through of my first draft with three beta readers in five months' time (insert specific date).

Breaking down your big goal(s) takes the pressure off such a mammoth task. Try saying your ultimate goal aloud to yourself and see if your pulse quickens or your heart starts pounding—committing to a dream/goal/resolution can be unnerving at first. We tend to get stuck in our happy(ish) daily rut and only ever let our imagination work on our behalf. If you've heard yourself saying "I would love to…" or "I wish I could…" then don't wonder or wish any more—commit to changing your life for the better, now! As the beautiful and inspirational Audrey Hepburn once said, "*Nothing is impossible, the word itself says, 'I'm possible.'*"

CELEBRATING ACHIEVEMENTS

From the outset, I was able to achieve my main goal of writing more because I'd chosen to blog the entire year's events—a great idea that came up thanks to using the mind map method. Writing about the challenge on such a public forum also ensured that I remained accountable for my goals. It was out there for the world to see, and if I failed, everyone would be watching.

That might sound a bit scary, but it had a motivational impact on me. Yes, I did fail at certain points throughout the year, but I blogged about it openly and received incredible feedback from readers who could relate to how I was feeling. There is absolutely nothing wrong with failure—it's how we learn and evolve.

Being accountable for your goals is a wonderful way to keep you focused and pushing for that success. You don't have to go to the extreme of blogging; you can simply tell two friends what you are doing and ask them to be supportive towards you.

One of the most important discoveries I made during my year-long journey was the value of celebrating my achievements—however small they might be. I always took a moment at the end of every month to write a summary post and absorb the implications of what I'd just achieved. In my first month's challenge, I lost ten pounds in weight; for month four, I gave up alcohol for thirty days. These weren't massive accomplishments, but they were important to me and meaningful for the voyage I was on. Observing the daily, weekly, monthly, or yearly progress that you make keeps you focused on your destination but allows you to enjoy the journey.

"Success is a journey, not a destination."

~ Arthur Ashe ~

Building confidence in yourself is vital for achieving success. So many of my friends, and the readers who meet me in person, tell me how impressed they are at the cool and calm persona I have and how self-assured I act. Do you want to know a secret? I fake it! One of my all-time favourite mantras for life is "fake it until you make it," and I've lived by this affirmation for a long time. It's not about deception or cheating the system. It's an inbuilt survival tool for getting stuff done. If I think about kicking off my blog, for example, I didn't have the faintest idea what I was doing when I started, but I began anyway. I did my research, learned everything I could from other bloggers along the way, and applied these lessons to my project—all the while writing and publishing content, marketing those posts across Twitter and Facebook, and "acting" like a blogger. No one questioned me; nobody pulled me up and said, "Hey, hang on, who do you think you are?" Why? Because I was blogging like a pro and providing the public with a service (content) that they were interested in reading.

Pretending to be confident when you're screaming inside is something, I'm sure, many of you have experienced at some point in your life. Whether it's walking into a crowded bar, talking in front of a boardroom full of people, starting a new job, learning a new skill, or meeting a prospective partner, we've all had to fake it a little bit at one time or another, so why not apply this to your goals? If you act as though writing a book is something you do every other day or like starting a business is a typical Monday morning to-do task, you're more likely to feel confident on the inside, which shines through and projects itself onto your expression, behaviour, stance, and voice. Remember—fake it until you make it!

"By prevailing over all obstacles and distractions, one may unfailingly arrive at his chosen goal or destination."

~ Christopher Columbus ~

SUMMARY

I hope you've found this chapter useful and have a lovely long list of things you want to do, have, or be. Maybe you've filled your notebook with page after page of mind maps in every colour of the rainbow—feel free to share them on my Facebook page www.facebook.com/MotivateMeBlog—or maybe you're still at that mulling it all over stage. Whatever phase you've reached, I want you to embrace it and feel excited about the journey you're about to take. These are exciting times!

Let's do a quick recap of what we've covered so far:

- You've given some thought to what you want to achieve over the next week/month/year and jotted down all the things you feel passionate about.
- In your notebook, you've had fun playing with the mind map technique and used this to expand on your ideas, create new topic threads, or discover your innermost desires.
- You've written a list of your favourite ideas and developed each one with its own mind map.
- Out of your list, you've chosen one/two/five/twelve tasks to explore further, used the SMART acronym to ensure that you know exactly how you will achieve each goal and worked out what the deadline will be for every item.
- Where necessary, you've broken down a big goal into smaller, more manageable chunks, so you don't feel overwhelmed.

Finally, you pulled up your big girl/boy panties and walked the walk, talked the talk, and faked it until you felt like the boss of your entrepreneurial paradise! Watch out Oprah, here comes ________________ (insert your name here).

PLANNING IS KEY

"All you need is the plan, the road map, and the courage to press on to your destination."

~ Earl Nightingale ~

I'M QUITE lucky in that I have a huge obsession with notebooks, calendars, diaries, workbooks, planners, pens, in fact, all stationery. It's a physical impossibility for me to walk past a Paperchase outlet and not buy something.

Most of my friends are tech mad, and so for them, it's all about the electronic gadgets and memo apps. I go out with my sister-in-law and our good friend Caroline every month, and when it gets to the end of the night we put a date in the diary for the next month's meetup. They both take out their phones and start scrolling for appropriate apps, whereas I pull out my A5 diary, an assortment of coloured pens, and a smiley face sticker, so I know it's a "fun activity." I do love my laptop, e-reader, and iPhone, but I love tactile stationery more.

When I was planning out my resolution challenge for *How I Changed My Life in a Year*, the paper tools came in very handy. I had a year-to-view wall planner where I could plan out my challenges and assign a day/date for all the relevant blog posts. At a glance, I knew exactly what I was going to be working on that week. Any panic or anxiety about the content I needed for a particular blog post disappeared once I looked at my planner.

I use this organisational tool every day of my life because it means my blog is well thought out and structured, and my marketing plan is actionable. When I came to the end of my yearlong challenge, I felt a bit deflated. I'd enjoyed writing the blog so much, and it had become such an integral part of my daily life that I didn't want it to end. After a few days of sulking, I realised it didn't have to—I just needed to adapt it and continue to post valuable content along a similar line as the challenge themes. It evolved into more of a motivational lifestyle blog and continued to do so with each passing year.

Planning became all the more important because the challenge had ended, and I was now pulling content out of thin air. Having an orderly system in place takes away that overpowering feeling of dread. What am I going to write about? When am I going to post it?

If you have settled on a particular resolution to work on over the coming months/years, using a wall planner or a diary helps you to stay focused on achieving your tasks. Breaking down your goal into pieces means that you will have several deadlines on the go at once. Write them down in bold. You only need to glance at your wall planner to spot a looming purple deadline, and it will spur you into action.

I mentioned taking part in NaNoWriMo earlier. In my paper diary, I have NaNo written in green pen on all the days in November that I can dedicate to writing for the contest. To stay on target, every participant needs to pen a minimum of 1,666 words a day for thirty days. Some days I might not be able to commit to this for one reason or another, so I'll scribble down on the next clear day *NaNo 3000+*, which gives me a clear indication of what I need to achieve.

There may be apps available that do the same thing; I can't comment nor recommend any because that's not how I choose to work. Feel free to use whatever fits in with your lifestyle. I know how helpful the visual, in-your-face wall planner technique is for me, but it might not be right for you. That's okay; adopt a system that suits you, but remember to update it regularly. To achieve anything in life, you must commit yourself 100 percent.

"I suggest that you become obsessed about the things you want; otherwise, you are going to spend a lifetime being obsessed with making up excuses as to why you didn't get the life you wanted."

~ Grant Cardone ~

I received wonderful feedback from hundreds of women across the globe following the publication of *How I Changed My Life in a Year*, and among the emails I received were several from readers who felt the urge to start their own blogs. Where possible, I followed their sites and commented on and shared the posts. Some of them are still going strong, but others have fallen away into the blogger graveyard. Why? It's down to planning. I know blogging was new to me when I wrote that first post, but the entire challenge, my goals, expectations, and basic content were prepared in advance.

I pictured my big goal—"complete my list of twelve New Year's resolutions by the end of the year and blog about it"—then I broke it down into smaller, monthly tasks, then I reviewed and updated each theme as I moved through the year. Remember—you can't trek up Machu Picchu without a plan.

On a smaller scale, I use a similar planning schedule for writing my books. As I now write full-time, it's imperative that I come up with new material on a regular basis. I'm not on an hourly rate here! I don't get paid for the days/months/years I sit at my desk writing. I only get paid once the editing is done and the book is published and promoted, and my dear readers very kindly purchase it.

I've created a project planner, which keeps me motivated and fixed on the deadlines. Working with editors, publishers, and cover designers means that I need to coordinate with them and submit my manuscripts at specific times throughout the year. For example, my editor has an eight-month waiting list, so I need to manage this by synchronising my planner to match her schedule.

Planning became a vital part of achieving success for my writing goals. Here is a rough guide to my book-writing planner. I open a new Excel spreadsheet on my desktop and add the project title. It might be something like "Write Two Books in a Year." Then I'll break my big project goal into sections and assign a month to each one, like this:

Outline Book One in January

Write Chapters 1–4 in February (approximately nine thousand words)

Write Chapters 5–8 in March

Write Chapters 9–12 in April

By the time we reach June, I should have twenty-four chapters of a first draft. I'll put this manuscript away for a few weeks and start outlining the second book using the same principles while I leave the other to marinate (I find it easier to spot errors and inconsistencies if I take a break before beginning my edits). My fiction novels are around the fifty to sixty thousand-word mark, so twenty-four chapters is roughly a complete manuscript. If I were writing a 120,000-word novel, then I'd continue working on the same book. Once the end of the year rolls around, I have two books in the draft stage, which I can then begin editing. Alongside the new books I'm working on, I will also be editing last year's manuscripts. It's an ongoing process that works for me, and I've become faster at producing work over the years. I use my spreadsheet as a motivational guideline as it shows me how I'm progressing with word count/chapters/timescale. If you want to start writing your first novel, don't place too much pressure on yourself to write four chapters a month; start with one and take it from there.

This project planner system works for many goals; you just need to adapt it to what you want to achieve. Having a clear and concise plan allows you to review your progress and make amendments much more easily than if you were winging it.

Let's look at another example where the project planner could be useful. What if you don't enjoy your current part-time administration job and long to start your own business to fit around your young family? You might be skilled with a needle and thread and be able to produce handmade baby and toddler gifts. For the past few years, you've made special, bespoke items for your friends, and they've been well received. Your big dream is to work from home selling your products.

Your project planner might look something like this:

- Project Title: Baby Boo Business.
- Outline business plan in January.
- Get professional guidance or advice from a trusted friend by the end of January at the latest. Commit to building a business with the aim of (or intention of) handing in notice at administration job by June.
- Build stock—start in January and continue throughout the year. Aim for four/five handmade pieces per month.
- Become active on social media from January, utilising the various hashtags. For example, #SolihullHour #CovHour #BrumHour. (NB: these tags are specific to the UK. If you are a resident elsewhere, then look for something similar in your town, city, or state.) This is another continuous task. Engage in relevant social media platforms, such as Instagram, Pinterest, and Face-

book. Join online networking groups and interact with other small businesses.

- Prepare sales/marketing literature in February. Have all research done by 20 February. Order business cards/flyers for delivery. Research local networking sessions.
- Sign up for networking groups in March. Make this a regular activity. Attend at least one session a month and take samples/flyers/business cards.
- Build an Etsy shop page/website in April. Update site weekly.
- Midyear review in June. Assess sales/stats to see if monthly income is sustainable to hand notice in at administration job and commit to a new business full-time.

That initial big goal to "Start a Business" could have been hugely daunting, but by breaking it down into manageable tasks and planning out the steps to take, it's not quite so scary anymore. In fact, if I were any good with a needle and thread, I'd be getting excited about this project. However, anyone who has seen my sewing skills will be thankful that this is just an example.

Think about other goals you could achieve using the project planner, such as weight loss, training for a marathon, or deciding on a new personal development training course.

When planning a project, I find it helpful to look at my life as a whole. Having a challenge plotted out is vital. The wall planner can be full of colourful action points and the diary overflowing with motivational quotes strategically written to keep focus; however, if you haven't made room for such a goal in your day-to-day life, then it can impact every area.

I happen to love lifestyle planners and weekly journals. They are the ideal place to write everything down that you need to remember. In the next section I talk more about organising your life, but for now, I want to touch briefly on how you currently spend the twenty-four hours you have in your day. When I did this exercise before starting the resolution challenge, I was amazed, and shocked, at how much free time I squandered. I realised that the old excuse of "I'd love to do XYZ, but I don't have the time" was absolute codswallop. The number of hours I wasted watching *Friends* reruns on TV was enough to motivate me to make drastic changes.

To work out how you spend your time during a day, have a go at this quick exercise. I promise you that it will focus your enthusiasm on making a few tweaks to your daily life. Grab a piece of A4 paper and a small plate. Draw around the plate, so you've got a large circle in the centre of your page. What you want to do is turn your circle into a clockface, so draw a cross through the centre from top to bottom and side to side. This represents the 12:00 (midnight), 6:00 a.m., 12:00 (noon), and 6:00 p.m. points. Now divide each quarter into six sections until you have the relevant numbered segments of a clockface. If you want to use the twenty-four-hour numbering system, then do so—whatever makes it easy for you.

Once you have your clock set up, you can start to fill in the sections. I used coloured pencils and shaded in the areas in different colours. For example, when I was asleep I shaded the relevant hours in blue, and when I was at work I coloured the slices in red. These two areas are probably going to be your biggest blocks of colour, as we sleep approximately seven to eight hours a day and work for around nine hours. For the remaining sections, divide them into your usual routines. When I did my clock, I had the following sections:

Breakfast/Shower/Dress the kids/ Pack schoolbags/
Prep school lunches

School run/Drive to work

Working

Lunch break

Drive home/School run

Football club/Swimming/Tae kwon do/Dance class

Dinner prep/Washing up

Kids homework/Bath time/Story/Bedtime

Ironing/Washing/Clearing up

Watching TV

Sleeping

Not a very inspiring list when it's written down, is it? In fact, when I first did this exercise it highlighted the fact that I was just existing and not living. When you colour in your segments and realise that you spend most of your time commuting or several hours a night rushing the kids to various after-school clubs, or see at a glance the amount of time you spend on household chores after a long day at work, it can be an eye-opening experiment.

After I saw my daily clock, I decided to make some changes. Some of them were simple tweaks that made a huge difference to my daily routine, such as making the kids packed lunches when I made the evening meal and putting them in the fridge. This saved at least twenty minutes every morning, as we could just grab them already prepared. Quitting the constant *Friends* reruns as I collapsed in front of the TV every night was another tweak that made a massive difference. I'd managed to get myself into a bad habit of just flopping on the sofa and flicking through the television channels. There wasn't anything specific I wanted to watch, so I just surfed, and in the process, I wasted approximately two to three hours a night. When I stopped watching telly at night, I found the time I needed to commit to my writing.

Now, I just want to point out that this might not work for everyone—I'm a single mum, don't forget, so I haven't got the pleasure of anyone's company once the kids are in bed. If you have a partner, then this time might be very precious to you both. Watching a television show together might be your time to chill out—do what's right for you and your lifestyle; only use my experiment as a guide.

One of the other changes I made impacted the children directly, but when I reviewed my decision, I realised it was the right thing to do for all of us. For about three years in a row, there wasn't a night of the week when I didn't have to run the kids to their various clubs. Having two boys and a girl means that they have different interests, so in the space of one week we would dash to tae kwon do on a Monday and Thursday, dance class on a Tuesday, swimming on a Wednesday, and football training on a Friday. At one point I could also throw cheerleading, Scouts, and tennis into that mix. It was a hard decision to make, but as my hands were riddled with eczema, my hair was going grey faster than I could dye it, and the bank balance was dwindling at an astonishing rate, I pulled them out of *all* their extracurricular classes.

As parents, we feel it oddly necessary to fill every waking moment of our child's life with something stimulating, challenging, and socially engaging—why? I did what every other parent I spoke to did; I ran around like a headless chicken, packing the kids in the car, dashing across town every night of the week, washing uniforms/kits, setting up direct debits, and sitting in the cold to watch them do whatever activity they were doing. When it stopped, I worried that my kids would be harmed in some way. I wasn't sure how, but surely by just staying at home night after night, I must be damaging their brains. As it turned out, that decision to pull back was spot-on. It gave us, as a family, several hours a week back to explore other activities, such as playing board games around the dinner table or, for the kids, riding out on their bikes with friends from up the road. They even, dare I say it, read a few books and messed around with arts and crafts. No lasting damage. There was another positive side effect of this time-saving plan, and that was how calm the house became. We were no longer thundering through the hall, swinging gym bags, football boots, or swimming kits around our heads. It was the best decision I ever made. As the kids have reached their teens, they have gone back to a few clubs; some of them are held at school and are run by teachers, others involve a few hours of standing on the side of a pitch, cheering on the U16s Sunday League football team. Times do change, and priorities alter, but when I needed it the most, I was able to find extra time in my day and week to work on other projects or dedicate to my family.

When you draw out your clockface, it might be the catalyst that spurs you on to change your job. Seeing a large block of colour eat into your day, especially if you're not enjoying your work, might be the push you need to focus on your action points—look for a new challenge, start a business, reduce your hours; whatever it is, this exercise will help you visualise a way forward.

As I mentioned at the start of this book, everything I've written about has been tried and tested by me. I use these tools all the time because I know they work. When I was preparing for my resolution challenge, I found these techniques invaluable. However, I don't want you to feel overwhelmed by all the information or the variety of exercises that I'm sharing. I use them, but it doesn't mean you have to. Pick one or two that you like the sound of and integrate them into your life. Try out a new method every month and see which one is the best fit. In the next section, I talk about lifestyle planning and how I managed to streamline my life to balance my work goals. Again, take from it what you need and discard the rest. My aim for writing this book was to share as much as I could to help motivate you to achieve success in any area of your life that you may need it.

I do hope, therefore, that you've found this section on planning helpful. Don't feel like you have to rush out and buy up all the writing materials in your local stationer's. Look around for an appropriate app if that's more fitting to your way of life. Using crayons, highlighters, and cheerful notebooks is a powerful tool in itself. Embracing your inner child can help in so many ways, and what better way of doing this than grabbing a piece of paper and drawing a picture? I don't mean a perfect landscape or an award-winning portrait (unless, of course, this is your forte). What I mean is draw like you would if you were five, or ten—stick figures and a square house with the door in the middle and four windows are perfect examples. I love doodling and often get carried away drawing eyes in all shapes and sizes. Being spontaneous and childlike in your artwork will trigger your inner child to come out and play, and this is when the magic of planning and goal setting can pay off.

The most important lesson in planning is to commit 100 percent to your goals. If you're not fully dedicated, you'll just be adding your ambition to the stack of unrealised resolutions.

"Dream it, live it, become it."

~ Shelley Wilson ~

ORGANISING YOUR LIFE

"Organise your dreams around your life and watch them come true."

~ Unknown ~

COMMITTING TO the mammoth resolution challenge I set for myself and dedicating twelve months of my life to achieving a string of tasks could be considered by some to be madness. Most sane people typically only pledge to complete one or two items on their New Year's resolution list, if that!

To be able to complete these goals, I knew I needed to look not just at the big yearlong project but at my life in general. Could I fit everything in? After all, I was a single mum with three children who demanded a certain amount of my time. I was also running my holistic health business and working five days and two evenings a week.

As my mum often tells me, if you want something done, ask a busy woman. I've found this to be true. When I look back over pockets of my life, I can't recall how I managed some of the things I did. For many years, I worked in the sales department of a prestigious hotel in Warwickshire. I worked four days a week and had to enrol my children in after-school clubs. I'd do a day's work, then ferry them to various extracurricular activities, help them with their homework, organise dinner, go through the kids' bedtime routines, and then begin my household chores. Don't get me wrong; that's nothing special, as I know there are gazillions of women and men doing the very same thing across the globe—but have you ever stopped to think "how the hell do we do it?"

The key to achieving success in anything we do is being organised. Every woman I know has a knack for multitasking in some way, whether that's juggling home and kids, managing a career and lifestyle, or perhaps dealing with a mix of all of the above. Organising your life and your goals takes away that bubbling panic and scatty brain fog that accompanies your overwhelming thoughts. Have you ever wanted to do something but couldn't quite verbalise your idea? Do you find that there are too many thoughts whirling through your brain and you find it difficult to ground yourself? Organisational techniques are vital in helping us calm the nerves and rationalise our feelings.

I talked about planning in the previous chapter and how writing down our goals can help us stay focused. I stand by this technique, as it's one of the main contributing factors for me achieving everything I set out to complete. But what about all the other stuff? While we plan out our incredible goals and prepare a project planner for our exciting new opportunities, who does the shopping? Who cooks all the meals? When does the bathroom get a decent scrub?

Nine times out of ten, our resolution list is abandoned because "real life" gets in the way. It might be our ultimate goal to shed two stone in weight, but notoriously, the third week of January is when we discard those promises we made to ourselves and scoff our way through the leftover mince pies. Our habits do have a lot to do with this self-sabotage, and I'm going to talk about that later, but for now, I want to share the basic techniques I used to streamline my life, organise my home, and take the stress out of everyday living, leaving me with plenty of spare time to commit 100 percent to my resolution challenge.

A GIRL'S GOTTA EAT!

I made the colossal mistake recently of doing my "big shop" at our local supermarket on a Saturday—never again! What is it with weekend shoppers? It's enough to stress out even the most laid-back individual. I'm sure even the Dalai Lama would lose it in the bread aisle on a Saturday afternoon.

"But we've got to eat, Shell!" I hear you cry. Yes, I agree, but why add so much anxiety to your already packed schedule? Wouldn't it be lovely to wake up on a Saturday morning and calmly glance over your planner, noting down a couple of action points you fancy doing, before taking the kids to the park or snuggling up on the sofa for a Netflix-a-thon? It *is* possible if you prepare yourself.

I'm going to start this organisational drive by looking at our most basic need—food. I love eating; I adore roast dinners, bacon butties, and pizza, but I detest cooking. Shopping comes a very close second to ironing as the job I would happily delegate for cold hard cash. So how on earth could I maintain my goals and cope with my resolution challenge *and* keep my children fed and watered?

There are two words that will change your life around entirely, and those words are "meal planner." I discovered the art of meal planning thanks to my Slimming World consultant, Julie. It's a conscientious goal to tell yourself you'll lose weight and eat healthily, but if you've had a bad day at work or been stuck on the motorway for four hours, then the last thing you want to do is start picking through the cupboards and fridge trying to work out what to cook the family for dinner.

To ensure we were all fed and didn't end up with a regurgitated menu of waffles, fish fingers, and baked beans, I spent an hour every Friday planning out the meals we would have for the coming week and writing a corresponding shopping list. It doesn't take long to do, and once you've got the hang of it, you might prepare two, three, or four weekly meal planners, so all you need to do is pick one and shop accordingly.

I list everything: breakfast, lunch, dinner, and any snacks. Here's one of my weekly meal planners to use as a guide. I must point out that the breakfast and lunch items are mine. My children have cereal or toast every morning, and during the week they have school dinners. The evening meals I make for the entire family. I'm lucky in that my kids have always enjoyed their food and eat most vegetables and aren't afraid of spice. You would choose meals that fit with your palate, culture, or lifestyle.

Monday

Breakfast: Porridge with Greek yogurt and fruit

Lunch: Potato salad with chicken

Dinner: Prawns and courgettes with pasta

Snacks: Fruit/Nuts

Tuesday

Breakfast: Porridge

Lunch: Soup and a roll

Dinner: Chicken in a tomato sauce, veg

Snacks: Fruit/Nuts

Wednesday

Breakfast: Mushroom omelette

Lunch: Fruit smoothie

Dinner: Sweet-and-sour pork with noodles

Snacks: Fruit/Nuts

Thursday

Breakfast: Porridge

Lunch: Chicken salad with peppers and red onion

Dinner: Cottage pie with sweet potato topping

Snacks: Fruit/Nuts

Friday

Breakfast: Porridge

Lunch: Soup and a roll

Dinner: Chicken pie, veg

Snacks: Fruit/Popcorn

Saturday

Breakfast: Bacon sandwich

Lunch: No crust vegetable quiche

Dinner: Prawn curry and rice

Snack: Fruit/Chocolate bar

Sunday

Breakfast: Scrambled eggs on toast

Lunch: Fruit smoothie

Dinner: Roast chicken, potatoes, veg, and gravy

Snacks: Fruit/Pudding with cream

Once I've worked out what we're going to eat, I write my shopping list. Some of the ingredients will be store cupboard items, so a quick glance will tell me if I need to replenish anything. Then I write down the fresh items I need: meat/fish, vegetables, fruit, dairy, and of course, I can't forget to add the everyday essentials to the list, such as toilet rolls, shampoo, and washing powder.

You might be reading this section and thinking to yourself, "I know how to shop, thank you very much!" That's great, and I'm not trying to teach you how to suck eggs here (no pun intended!), but there are a large number of people out there who would never think to plan their meals and coordinate their shopping lists, yet those same people are desperate to achieve their goals or change their lives, so this section is to help them streamline the mundane and smash the ordinary, and allow them the freedom to be exceptional.

Meal planning in advance was a huge help during my year of challenges. It was one less thing I had to worry about. As well as planning our menus and coordinating my shopping list, I also ordered everything online. Thank goodness for online grocery shopping. You can have your entire list uploaded in less than half an hour, saving your favourites so it's even faster the next time you log in. From the comfort of your home, still in your pyjamas, with a steaming cup of tea and a chocolate biscuit, you can accomplish your grocery shopping stress free and then sit back and wait for your delivery. It astounds me how many people don't take advantage of this facility. It's a wonderful feature and saves you a huge amount of time, effort, and money. Nearly every supermarket now offers online shopping, so if you don't already use this service, consider giving it a go.

I'm going to dare to take you deeper into my uber-organised life and tell you how to snatch back even more leisure time, which means more time to concentrate on your goals. Meal planning and online shopping are life-changers in themselves, in my opinion, but you can become the queen (or king) of orderliness by setting aside a few hours on the weekend to batch cook. Yep, you heard that right. I, the founding member of the "I hate cooking" crew, love a batch-cooking session. Who would have thought it?

I have The Body Coach legend, Mr. "easy on the eye" Joe Wicks to thank for this top tip. His advice for achieving success on his ninety-day shift, shape, and sustain plan is to spend one day (typically a Sunday) cooking up a storm and preparing several meals for the freezer. In one afternoon, I made ten main meals. Not only did I then have a clear plan of the food we would eat for the coming week and a fridge and cupboard full of supplies, but I had all the meals pre-prepared and stored in the freezer, so all I had to do was defrost them throughout the day and reheat for dinner. One day of cooking saved me approximately four hours of slaving over a hot stove across the seven days in a week. That's four hours of writing time, four hours to work on a business plan, four hours to be creative with your dream. I'd say that's an organisational skill worth trying, wouldn't you?

PLEASE DON'T WRITE IN THE DUST

I hope you found the meal planning section helpful. I can't stress enough how much it's helped me over the years, not just while I was doing my resolution challenge but every week since. It became a habit and now only takes me a couple of hours a week to get all our menus planned, shopped for and precooked. I have so much more time to dedicate to other activities, work on my writing projects, and be with my family.

However, I do have bad days and off weeks where the planning goes out the window, my motivation slumps, and the house dissolves into chaos—I am only human after all. Yet, having these techniques at my disposal means that when I get my head back in the game I can pick up where I left off and start over. I'm not looking at a total overhaul, just a tweak to get back on track.

Food and cooking go hand in hand with my next organisational tip: dealing with household chores. Keeping on top of the washing, ironing, cleaning, and gardening can feel like a full-time job in itself.

As a single mum I don't have another adult around to offer a helping hand, so ever since my children were young, I have tried to instil in them a desire to keep their bedrooms clean and tidy. As I'm sure every mother reading this book can confirm, it's a battle I'll never win. So, what do I do? I close the bedroom door and walk away. For years it would wind me up to see the clothes strewed across the floor, the towels festering in the corners, and the increasing number of plates and cups that would occupy the desk instead of homework. My blood pressure would go through the roof when I caught a whiff of last week's football socks, still languishing on the chair instead of in the wash basket, which was five inches to the left.

My middle son helped me to reach my walk-away attitude when I was once again nagging him to clear up. His response to my "Why can't you just sort this mess?" was short yet succinct, "But it's *my* room." He was right; as teenagers, it's imperative that they have their own space, regardless of how many species of fungi might be growing up the walls. So, I walked away. Ever since I made the decision to leave their rooms alone, I've spotted one or more of my teens carrying the vacuum upstairs at various times of the month and returning with bin bags full of rubbish. Miracles clearly do happen.

Our homes are more than just the kids' rooms, however, and if you are brave enough to leave your children to manage their mess, then you only need to concentrate on the other areas. The tip I'm about to share with you only took off in our house towards the end of my challenge year—in November to be exact. I mentioned in an earlier chapter how anxious and excited I was about taking part in NaNoWriMo. Blocking out periods of time in my diary meant that I could commit to that project wholeheartedly. However, the school uniforms still needed to be washed and ironed, I still wanted the bathroom to be clean, and I knew that the kids wouldn't be able to resist writing rude words in the dust if I didn't keep on top of it.

I required some help, and I realised long ago that if I didn't ask for it, then life would tick along with "good ole mum" sorting everything out regardless of how many projects I had on the go at any one time. My children were old enough to hold an iron, flick a duster, and even mow the grass, so it was time to cash in on their talents. Money may have been mentioned briefly—something along the lines of "If you want any pocket money this week, you're going to have to pull your finger out." To make it fair, I broke up all the household chores and split them into quick-fix tasks. Then I assigned a couple of duties to each day. I've got a chalkboard in the kitchen with the list written on it, so we all know what needs doing and when on any specific day. Here's what our most basic chore list looks like:

Monday

Polish downstairs rooms

Mop kitchen floor

Laundry

Tuesday

Clean bathroom

Polish upstairs rooms

Take bins out

Wednesday

Vacuum downstairs rooms

Laundry

Fish tank

Thursday

Vacuum upstairs rooms

Clean toilet

Friday

Ironing

Laundry

Saturday

Clean kitchen

Sunday

Ironing

Laundry

Meal prep

As I was working full-time and attempting to achieve numerous assignments every week, I found that I ended up spending the majority of my weekend cleaning, washing, and ironing instead of having fun, blogging, or working on my other projects. Discovering this technique to manage the household stuff was a lifesaver. When my chore list said, "laundry" I put one wash load on. Within one week I was up to date with the washing pile and have kept it low ever since. When the board said, "ironing", I'd do an hour at a time—just enough to keep the kids in uniforms and me in jeans and jumpers.

Dealing with the house in small sections at a time keeps everything flowing well. There are other tasks I add in when required. The bigger jobs like windows, bedding, and decluttering I slot in at various times throughout the month, but on the whole, I know the house is being cleaned and regularly tidied without me busting a lung and wasting my weekend. The kids get involved by picking one or two jobs to do to earn their pocket money. They are pretty good with the vacuum, and my middle son is fabulous at ironing.

Once again, just like the meal planning, our chore list has become a habit, and it's not something we stress over or even think about obsessively. It just gets done, and more importantly, there are no sibling squabbles over who does what task.

Think about your job, be it full or part time, and the hours you spend in the evening, or on weekends, cleaning up after everyone else. Now go back to your notebook and look at the mind maps you created, glance at all the wonderful goals you wrote down, remember the passion you felt when you thought about starting a new business, writing a book, or changing your life for the better. Which would you rather be doing: ironing for four hours or project planning, scrubbing the bathroom or researching premises for your new shop? Only you can make the changes happen.

If you have a family, get them involved. Teaching our children to be responsible, helpful, and independent is a life skill that will stay with them, so why not start now? A two-year-old can hold a duster, and with a bit of teamwork, you could have fun doing the housework together. Even if you are single and live by yourself, adopting these habits will give you more leisure time to go out with friends, and concentrate on working towards your dreams. Perhaps you're lucky and still live at home with your parents. If that's the case, there's no harm in volunteering your services, so you start creating positive habits—one day you'll have that first home and a new set of skills to take with you. Welcome this new organised life, and don't be afraid to explore other ways to save time and energy.

DECLUTTERING FOR THE MIND, BODY, AND SPIRIT

Decluttering is one of my favourite pastimes. I have a regular clear-out once a month, and yet, for a reason I'm still struggling to understand, our family has a knack for attracting *stuff* in a constant stream. Sorting out the piles of magazines, old clothes, and other household paraphernalia is not only virtuous—who wants to be falling over heaps of useless rubbish every day—it's also incredibly therapeutic.

I dedicated an entire section to decluttering in *How I Changed My Life in a Year*, and it's the one topic I receive the most messages about. It appears I'm not the only one who hoards.

The reason I wanted to talk about it in this book is that the process of decluttering links in perfectly with successful project planning. In the world of holistic health and personal development, the *stuff* we fill our homes with has energy attached to it—good and bad. Think about an object you own: a vase, a piece of jewellery, artwork. When you see it, wear it, or use it you may experience feelings of joy, pride, or nostalgia. That energy seeps into everything in the environment, and your feelings are amplified, also impacting the space and people around you. It's not a problem if this article has beneficial emotions attached to it, but what if that item is negative and a reminder of less fortunate times or a life-changing period in your life? Do you want to be constantly reminded about the bad times?

Before starting a new project, setting your goals, or embarking on a career change, it's wise to allow yourself a few hours, days, or weeks to sort through specific areas in your home and clear the clutter. Energy stagnates around mounds of mess, and if the energy isn't moving, then we start to feel lethargic, anxious, and stuck. That's not a helpful way to feel if you're about to start a new challenge. We need to be feeling positive, powerful, and excited. Remember what I said about being 100 percent passionate about our goals? Well, we not only need to plan and organise ourselves; we need to make our lives as streamlined and fresh as we can.

Like many homes in the UK, we have a cupboard under the stairs. As much as I would love to say it houses a small wizard, I'm afraid it is actually a dumping ground for shoes, bags, and anything else that needs to be quickly moved out of sight if the doorbell rings. As my stairs are fairly central in my house, this means the cupboard is right in the centre of my home's floor plan. In feng shui terms, it means the small cupboard under the stairs relates to our health, unity, and well-being. So, if it's full to the brim with muddy football boots, old shoes, and empty bags, what do you think that is doing to our energy?

I am fascinated by feng shui—the art of balancing and harmonising the flow of natural energy in our environment (work or home) for the benefit of our well-being. It didn't become popular in the West until the 1970s, but it's a practice that has been used for centuries in China. It's also understood that feng shui can be traced back to many ancient civilisations, such as the Aztecs, Indians, and the Egyptians. Even though I don't know nearly enough about the principles and technical workings of feng shui, I have been able to use some of the philosophies in my life, and I've reaped the benefits.

Clearing the cupboard under the stairs has a remarkable impact on me, my health, and the atmosphere in our house—I can't explain it; I just know it works. So, if I feel myself getting a bit stuck with a project, I'll declutter, and I'll always start under the stairs. If you fancy learning more about the art of clearing your clutter, I can recommend *Clear Your Clutter with Feng Shui* by Karen Kingston. It's a fabulous little book—easy to read and even easier to implement.

The disorder in our home or office isn't the only thing we need to declutter to help us achieve success. There are numerous other ways to reorganise your life and accommodate all the good vibes and exciting opportunities and to embrace your new challenges. What I'm about to share might seem odd, or even scary, but I'm talking from experience when I reveal these tips.

Cutting back on your social media might seem like the most horrific thing I've suggested to you so far, but I don't want you to panic. I'm one of the most obsessive users of Facebook and Twitter and have no intention of letting up. However, I have decluttered my pages (yes, I have more than one) several times over.

Let's start with Facebook. It's a wonderful tool to use for interacting with family, friends, and like-minded individuals. You can have a personal page, and business pages to advertise your unique services. I have a personal page and two business pages—one for my blog (www.facebook.com/MotivateMeBlog) and one for my young adult fantasy fiction (www.facebook.com/FantasyAuthorSLWilson). The nature of my business means that I must maintain an online presence; otherwise the world won't know I exist, and won't learn about my books, blog, or events.

On my personal page, I have a mix of friends who I haven't seen face-to-face in over ten years, ex–work colleagues, school friends, and my best buds. Some of my connections live overseas, and Facebook is, therefore, the only way I have to stay in constant contact. My family lives two hours away in Yorkshire, but I get to follow their lives via our online link. There are so many positive points about social media, but there are also the negatives. I'm not going to dwell on the darker side of Facebook, but what I do want to share is how I regularly declutter my personal page and unfriend or unfollow everyone who is a negative drain.

I don't tolerate anyone who spams me or tries to sign me up for groups I'm not interested in or sell me something without first interacting in a positive way. The number of people who have sent me a friend request, and within seconds of me clicking the "confirm as friend" button have hurled me a message to join their growing business selling juice/horse manure/enema kits is astounding. What do I do? I hit unfollow faster than I can devour a Wispa bar. I love interacting with people; I thrive on getting to know my community and sharing their highs, relating to their lows, and engaging positively—*that's* what Facebook is all about for me.

Decluttering your Facebook page is a must. You want to be interacting with like-minded people, encouraging individuals and companies that are in alignment with your vision and life. It's important that you are using this social site to help you achieve success in your given area. For example, I'm a member of quite a few groups on Facebook; some of them are networking mums and local businesses, and others are authors or book bloggers. I've attended loads of face-to-face meetups off the back of these groups and have made some incredible new friends who support me, my business, and my books—both online and in person.

Twitter is another favourite of mine. However, I don't use this site for friends and family. For me, Twitter is all about my blog and books. I follow authors, bloggers, marketing companies, local businesses, some celebrities (I know, I know, but I couldn't resist—Ian Somerhalder is just so damn cute). From a business perspective, Twitter is the leading source for my blog traffic. In other words, most of my blog readers found my articles because of a tweet I wrote or a tweet another follower retweeted/shared. It's like a huge online word-of-mouth network. One mistake that quite a few Twitter users make is to fixate on the stats. They can even go as far as buying followers to make them look popular. I've never understood this as I like to generate my followers organically. I like to know who I'm following and ensure that we all interact in a mutually beneficial way. For example, I share quite a few tweets from other authors, regardless of what genre they write in. Romance novels aren't my thing, but half of my followers might love a romance, and therefore I'll share what I think they might be interested in. Using the lists feature means that I can keep organised and divide the accounts I follow into specific areas, so they are easy to find.

Following anyone and everyone who clicks on your page isn't going to generate a positive relationship, so decluttering your Twitter followers in the same way you would on Facebook keeps you focused on the positive aspects of your social media accounts.

These principles can be applied to all the social sites you engage with: Pinterest, LinkedIn, Snapchat, Instagram, Tumblr, StumbleUpon, among others.

If you've been brave and stuck with me through the social media declutter, then grab yourself a reward—you deserve it. When I started my resolution challenge, it was important that I connected with people who found my project interesting. The people I engaged with have become my regular readers and interact with me on a daily or weekly basis. That's what you want to aim for. There's no point spending hours online chatting to dog lovers if you've got five cats.

Another area that benefits from decluttering, but might make you just as nervous, is your real-life friendships/relationships. We all have friends who drain us of positive energy after an hour, or who are larger than life and make us feel like utter failures. Re-evaluating your friendships is just as important for your sanity as it is for your success, but we don't tend to consider this aspect unless we've reached a turning point in our lives.

At various points over the years, I've made friends with people who have played a huge role in my life and then disappeared. Sometimes they are replaced by other people, and other times they leave a black hole of regret and sorrow. Occasionally, you put all your trust in one friend or in a group of friends who let you down when you need them the most. As difficult as it might be to recognise this, it's imperative that you *do* accept it. They are no longer a good fit for where you are heading, and as heartbreaking as it may be, life moves on, and you meet other people who are on the same, or a similar, path as you. Invest your time and energy in friendships that matter; help who you can, and along the way, they will help you tread your path, influence your decisions, or offer sound advice when it is needed.

Maintaining certain relationships is also vital. You'll instinctively know who matters and who you can call on to talk about business plans, your goals, and challenges, or who will happily listen to you vent for an hour. As I reached my forties, I realised how significant it was to have a smaller group of excellent friends instead of hundreds of acquaintances. Nurture the friendships that matter; release the ones that drain or upset you.

SELF-CARE PLAN

Every day is full of hope, health, and happiness.

I'M A great believer in the body/mind/spirit loop. What we think can be manifested in our lives, as well as our physical bodies. It's relatively easy to talk yourself into an illness if you mention it often enough. When I was finally diagnosed with depression several years ago, I didn't help myself because I slumped into a spiral of negative thought. If I'd turned that negativity around, I might not have suffered so deeply or for as long as I did. Depression is a frightening thing to experience, and as a chemical imbalance, it can be nearly impossible to stop it once the fog descends; however, I found that the severity of an attack was dependent on my inner dialogue.

When I decided to set my resolution challenge I knew I had to keep myself in tip-top shape so the year went well. It amazes me how easy it is to achieve your goals when you are in optimum health and feeling passionate about your day. But how can you keep yourself fit and healthy, run a home/business/life, and still have energy left to commit to the changes you want to make in life and the challenges you want to achieve? In this section, I want to talk about the self-care plan I put in place during my yearlong quest. Take from it what you need and discard the rest. Your life is unique to you, and it's therefore up to you what, how, and when you look after yourself.

I was able to achieve so much in twelve months because I followed a variety of self-care techniques. Most of these I learned over my years as a holistic health practitioner; others I stumbled across thanks to recommendations from friends. I'll share it all, and you decide if it suits you and your lifestyle. One of the developmental tools I believe in most is allowing yourself a reward when you achieve something important. For example, when I finished my second-month challenge, which saw me leaping around like a maniac on the Wii Fit, cycling, walking, and skipping, I booked myself in for a lava shell massage before I started on month three.

We talked about celebrating achievements earlier, and this is a perfect way to do that. Allocate prizes for yourself when you arrive at certain points in your goals. If you've decided to write a book, purchase a new pen or notebook when you finish your first draft. Maybe you've decided to lose weight or join the gym; it might not be wise to include a tube of Pringles or a bottle of rioja as a bonus in these circumstances, but a massage, new dress, or night at the theatre would be a huge incentive.

It helps us to focus on what we want to accomplish if there is some booty at the end of the journey. Now, if your goal is to start a new business, getting that first sale might be reward enough. That's fine, do what feels right. If it's a change of job, then a new outfit for your first day might be just what you need to feel confident and positive about the exciting chapter you are about to embark upon. Large or small, cheap or expensive; the decision is up to you as to how you reward yourself—just make sure it's enough of an incentive to keep you going.

Let's look at some of the treats you can allocate yourself when you reach the finish line each month.

BODY

A back, neck, and shoulder massage is incredibly helpful when you've been hunched over a computer screen for hours at a time. So if your goal is to write a book or start a blog, then this is the self-care plan for you.

They say music feeds the soul. I'd have to agree with that, as having a ten-minute dance around the kitchen is enough to release those feel-good hormones and motivate you into action. Maybe your musically themed self-care session is buying a new album, booking tickets to see your favourite band, or going to a musical.

Laughter is advantageous for the body, the mind, and the soul. Watching a comedy on TV or going to the cinema can be an inspiring treat. Or perhaps a night out with friends at your local comedy club would be a better choice. I often book myself in for a coffee and chat with those friends who always make me laugh—this is one of my favourite rewards and benefits everyone involved.

We can't talk about self-care for the body without referring to some of the most popular vices—wine and chocolate. If you've achieved an important goal or reached a deadline and feel immensely proud of yourself, then grab that chocolate bar or have that large glass of wine—you deserve it.

It might seem strange to include a gym session as a bonus for doing well. However, I know from experience how miserable I feel before hitting the gym compared to the euphoria and high energy levels I have when I've finished my session. So yes, you can count it as a reward. Going for a swim, taking part in a dance class, or having a workout boosts your mood and strengthens your body—everything you want to achieve to keep you in tip-top shape.

I enjoyed a slap-up roast chicken dinner after completing a meat-free week during my resolution challenge. Your rewards don't have to be expensive or elaborate.

I can't talk about self-care without sharing a few lines about alternative therapies and holistic health; after all, this is where my heart belongs. There are so many remedies available to help you not only maintain your well-being but assist you in the planning and organisational side of setting your goals and achieving success. I already mentioned the benefits of feng shui for keeping you focused in the previous chapter. It's utilising these techniques that will change your life. Here's a quick review of my favourite holistic therapies that you might want to try out:

- Reiki—the natural healing process in the body is activated when a practitioner uses hands-on energy healing. A deeply relaxing treatment carried out while you are fully clothed.
- Reflexology—a practitioner works on specific points on your feet, which correspond to every part of your body, effectively balancing your entire system.
- Acupuncture—fine needles are inserted into various points on the body, called meridians (energy lines), to treat a variety of physical and mental issues.
- Massage—the muscles in the body are manipulated to relieve tension and stress.

Think about other things you can do that will reward your body: going for a walk, taking a nap, soaking up the sun. Whatever you enjoy doing, add it to your notebook under the title of Self-Care Plan.

MIND

It is important to look after our physical body, and if you are working hard on accomplishing your targets, then a massage, nap, or glass of wine will support your efforts. However, it is equally important to provide a self-care plan for our mind.

When we are working flat out on our objectives, it can put an added strain on our poor brains. There is always an inner dialogue flowing, and if you're anything like me, it rarely shuts up. That's where a reward for the mind is so successful. Giving our overworked and wired minds a time-out has a knock-on effect for productivity and inspiration. Here are my favourite self-care options for the mind:

Start a happiness pot. I have a mason jar, which is decorated with stickers and glitter glue, in my kitchen. Inside are tons of small folded pieces of paper. On each one, I've written something fabulous that happened to me. Here are a few examples from my pot:

- Winning the Most Inspirational Blog award and travelling to London to pick up my prize and meeting hundreds of other bloggers
- Appearing in the Writers' Forum magazine on a double-page spread
- Having lunch with my sister-in-law and going with her to collect my nephew from school
- Joining a creative writing class at my local college

I start it on New Year's Day and add to it over the twelve months and then on New Year's Eve I tip it out and reread all the incredible things I've achieved/done/enjoyed.

Have a 100 percent selfish day. My good friend and fellow author, Peter Jones, who wrote *How to Do Everything and Be Happy*, doesn't restrict himself to only having Boxing Day on 26 December. In addition to enjoying the annual festive holiday, he gives himself extra Boxing Days at various times throughout the year. He encourages you to call these days whatever you want. I call mine "Shelley Time." Peter talks about the simplicity of an old-fashioned Boxing Day when the shops were closed, there were great films on the television, and the day was spent in total relaxation. What's stopping us from recreating this on a monthly, or quarterly, basis? He adds it to his calendar and diary, blocks out the entire day, and then uses those twenty-four hours to do whatever he wants. If he fancies a duvet day to read a book or watch a box set, he does that; if he decides that he wants to jump on a train and head to the seaside, he does. There are no rules, apart from being spontaneous and sticking to it. I use Peter's Boxing Day technique quite often but adapt it to make sure I'm still around for the kids. You can make it work the best way for you, but taking an entire day to do whatever the hell *you* want is a fabulous way to reward yourself.

Meditate. One of my favourite self-care projects for the mind is meditation. Taking just ten minutes to be still, quiet, and calm is enough to recharge your batteries and enjoy your day. I adore the Headspace app, which I downloaded on my phone. Andy Puddicombe, leading mindfulness and meditation expert and founder of Headspace, has one of the best meditation voices around. I could listen to him all day.

Turn off your gadgets. Another way to declutter the mind is to aim for a tech-free hour/day/night. Turn off your phone, TV, and laptop and do something else, away from technology. Breathing exercises or a walk in the park—do something that takes you away from the constant buzz of electronics. I've started leaving my phone in another room after 7:00 p.m., so I can be fully present for my kids. Not hearing the constant ping, pong, twang, and fizz of the various notifications is hugely beneficial for the mind.

SPIRIT

Everything that's good for the body and mind will be good for the soul. As I mentioned earlier, there is a brain/body/spirit loop that connects everything we think and do. So, what can you do that will reward your soul? That's easy; try one of these:

- Enjoy a meal out with family/friends and relish the companionship and face-to-face conversation.
- Take up knitting. When I attempted knitting for the first time during my resolution challenge, I realised that I was the world's worst knitter. At least I had a go, and as a reward, I opted for an adult colouring book—I can keep inside the lines on paper; I'm just dreadful at sticking to straight lines with wool.
- Get a pet. The benefits of having a pet are constantly in the media. Stroking a dog, cat, rabbit, or another such fluffy companion is hugely beneficial for calming your mind and body. When I was ill and struggling with my symptoms, I found great comfort in snuggling up with our then kitten. She has since grown up into a mischievous cat but still loves a cuddle now and then, and surprisingly, if I'm ever feeling under the weather or weeping at a sad film, she'll come and sit with me. It's like she's offering herself up for my self-care plan.
- Help someone. This is a marvellous way to feed your soul. Popular book reviewer and fellow blogger, Rosie Amber, spent a few years blogging about her experiences of doing a good deed every day for two years. Some were small tasks, such as filling a charity bag, and others were more detailed, such as going to a local school and listening to children read. The sheer joy you get from helping someone else is a huge reward for the soul—add it to your self-care plan.

As you see, the rewards don't have to be expensive, elaborate, or complicated to arrange. Just make sure you allow yourself a little luxury now and then to keep you motivated on achieving the big goal. Write down your favourite self-care options in your notebook and then add one a month to your calendar, diary, or app. Make a date for yourself and enjoy it.

It's probably worth noting here that self-care is *not* selfish or self-centred. Looking after yourself should be at the very core of who you are. I've known people to shy away from treating themselves because they feel guilty; I've also known women who burn out completely because they gave everything they had to their family and didn't take care of themselves. When you take care of how you feel, inside and out, it has a knock-on effect on everyone around us: our family, friends, and the environment. We end up doing everything in a healthier and more effective way.

I read a marvellous article many years ago where the author believed that giving too much of oneself was a sign that a vital need wasn't being met or an emotion wasn't being expressed. I could relate to that article so well. Back then, I was married and miserable, I did everything I could for my children because I couldn't speak up about the abuse, and I was receiving no love from my husband. I was yearning for a more meaningful relationship, love, friendship, and respect. Instead, I lived my life in trepidation, fear, and anguish. After I had walked away from that life, I began to understand the importance of looking after myself first. There are numerous ways to test yourself and see if you are resistant to including a few treats in your goal-setting plans. Do you often say "I don't have time to…" or maybe you say "No one appreciates what I do." In truth, you're saying "I don't value myself enough to take the time to…" or "I do too much in the hope that someone will notice me." It can be quite a challenge in itself to test yourself like that, but it's a valuable exercise. Changing how you think can help you accept the benefits of self-care. Jot down in your notebook the answers to the following questions:

- What do I need right now?
- What could I do without?
- What or who is making me feel resentful? Why?

Answering these questions can help you work out where you feel deprived in life, and then you can start to correct those feelings. It could be one of your action points for a goal you want to achieve.

Let's put it into practice so you can see how positive this exercise can be. In the previous chapter we talked about delegating household chores, and we worked out an organisational plan to get the jobs done quickly and efficiently over the week. Imagine now that one of the reasons you can't take advantage of a self-care treat is because you have to do all the cleaning, cooking, washing, and ironing. This is the perfect time to implement that household chore planner. It's the right opportunity to say "I need someone to clean the bathroom every week and, when I'm not here, put the next load in the washing machine." Doesn't that sound better than "I have to do everything around here," which is as good as saying "I don't ask for help"?

From now on I want you to try to recognise when you are using the negative language of deprivation and try to turn it around. Appreciate that self-care is paramount to your well-being and success. In turn, by looking after ourselves, we also teach our children how important it is to look after their own needs—something that will stay with them into adulthood. There has been a rise in articles published in the press about the huge increase in mental health issues for children as young as six or seven. It is vital that they understand that embracing self-care is a must. Let's teach our children how to be strong, courageous, and well-rounded adults, so they can pay it forward to the next generation, and so on.

YOUR CHEERLEADING SQUAD

It took me a long time to ask people for help when I needed it, but when I did, I realised how open and willing people are to offer their assistance. Don't be afraid to seek help when working on a goal that is important to you. The cheerleading analogy came to me after my daughter joined a local dance group several years ago. These girls worked hard every week on their routine and were able to showcase their talents at local fetes and events in the borough. They would create a human pyramid in time to the music and delight the audience with colourful pom-poms, outfits, and aerial acrobatics as they flung the lightest of the group, the *flyer*, through the air by her feet.

As I watched the group perform at a local event, I noticed how the girls arranged themselves to provide the flyer with the most support and stability. There were four bases; normally these were the older girls with experience and confidence who held the baseline and kept the pyramid grounded. Then came the middle layer: girls who gave the flyer their undivided attention. Finally, there was the flyer; she was usually the smallest member of the group who handed total control of life and limb to her cheerleading squad. She was confident that the bases would support her, and the middle layer of girls would lift her up, and that as a team, they would make it back to the ground in one piece. I was in awe as I watched the perfect choreography and realised how easy life would be if we adopted the same strategy.

Take a moment to think about your family, friends, or colleagues. Who would be in your pyramid base? I know for a fact that my parents would be in mine, holding the line and supporting me 100 percent. I'm also fortunate to have a couple of friends who I can call on at any time, day or night, who would complete that baseline.

How about your middle layer? Who do you know that might not be a regular feature in your everyday life but would support anything you do? There are quite a few people I meet up with, and although

I only see them occasionally, they always support my events, book releases, and various other projects throughout the year—they are my middle layer, lifting me up.

It's an interesting exercise to work out who would form your cheerleading pyramid, and it can also help you clear away any negative influences, such as those we discussed earlier in the decluttering section. If you are flying through the air, you want to know that you're surrounded by the right kind of people.

"Surround yourself with people who reflect how you want to feel inside. Energy is real and it is contagious."

~ Massy Arias ~

NETWORKING GROUPS

Your cheerleading squad tends to be people you know reasonably well, but there are also many groups you can be a part of that offer just as much support as your best friends can.

Networking is a relatively new thing for me. When I ran my holistic health business, I worked five days and two evenings a week, so any spare time that I had I divided between family, friends, and my writing. Attending any of the networking groups in my local area was an impossibility. Once I closed that business and focused on my books and blog content, I discovered a necessity to get out of the home office and speak to another human being.

Working from home, in any capacity, has a host of benefits, from holding a conference call in your pyjamas, to saving hours on a long commute. Many mums I know are starting small businesses from their kitchen table to enable them to keep childcare costs to a minimum and reap the advantages of being around for their child's early years.

With this influx of mumpreneurs, the need for friendly and supportive networking groups is greater than ever. Women empower women; it's a beautiful thing to witness and an even more satisfying thing to do.

The groups I attend are primarily targeted at women in my local area. There are numerous networking meetings that are tailored to specific industries, such as coaching, design, sales, and marketing, but I needed to find a group that contained my target audience. As an author of self-help and personal development books aimed at women aged thirty plus, these smaller groups met my personal, professional, and marketing needs.

Since I also write a motivational blog, it is essential that I mix with the women I hope to help and evolve my blog into a lifestyle/goal-setting/organisational platform to help my audience be the best they can be, motivate themselves, and achieve great success. To achieve this, I needed first of all to find these ladies and then to discover how I could assist them with appropriate content and products.

Even though I'm a paper and pen kind of girl, I understand that connecting online is vital in today's society as we are all so busy. Being able to stay in touch with the click of a mouse saves valuable time and also keeps us grounded in real life. I'm a member of quite a few Facebook groups with a variety of themes, from book reviewers, bloggers, and authors, to well-being and health pages. I've also made some firm friends via these groups and even met up in person with several of the members. However, the online world can be a lonely one, and the positive benefits of face-to-face interaction are well-documented. Maintaining a mix of local networking groups held in a favourite café and social media groups can provide you with sufficient support.

Embracing everything that a networking group has to offer is fundamental to your growth, in a business and as a member of the community. Not only are you making valuable contacts, you are also creating lasting bonds with women who understand your anxieties, your nervousness, and your achievements.

The networking groups I attend lean heavily towards empowering small business owners. The monthly meetups are a great resource and will not only help advance fellow entrepreneurs but will also have a knock-on effect on your well-being: mentally, professionally, and spiritually. There are also groups out there that are tailored more for emotional support, such as MS networking associations or Women's Aid groups.

Explore all avenues in your area that offer networking opportunities, and use my top five tips as a guide for choosing the right group for you:

1. Most groups will have a Facebook page or a website. Take a few minutes to familiarise yourself with the setup, and look at the number of members who attend the meetings. If the group only attracts one or two people to their meetups every month, then it might be worth looking elsewhere. You want a networking session with the potential to interact with plenty of people.
2. Prepare any flyers/business cards/products for your business and take these with you. At all good group sessions, you will have the opportunity to introduce yourself, talk briefly about your business, and give out your literature to any interested parties.
3. Be supportive of one another. You may attend a networking group where the majority of members deliver the same, or similar, products. You might discover that the lady sitting next to you manufactures almost identical merchandise. Don't think of this person as a competitor—you will have separate customers, and probably

deliver to different areas. However, the opportunity to collaborate can provide huge benefits for you both.

4. Engage with each other once the meeting has ended. It's a great way to spend a couple of hours on a rainy Monday morning, but chatting about business over a latte doesn't end there. Exchange details, like each other's Facebook pages, and connect on Twitter or Instagram. Keep the lines of communication open and continue to interact in the future. I met some of my best friends at networking events. By joining in with conversations on their pages, supporting their businesses, and promoting their services to your audience, you might be able to help boost their profile and sales, and in turn, they will reciprocate.
5. Occasionally, you'll find a networking group who offers a bit more. They may have a members' club or a closed group on Facebook where they share additional content. Look into this opportunity and join in when or where appropriate. There is normally an annual fee. For example, in the UK this tends to be anywhere between £50–£100 a year. The group leader will be able to tell you what benefits you get for your money, so don't be afraid to ask. These advantages might be just what your small business needs to advance and grow.

The best advice I can give you is to enjoy yourself. Meeting other small business owners/like-minded individuals is a delight, as you have so much in common. It doesn't matter whether you attend to sell a product; chat about marketing plans, sales techniques, and promotional aspects of your business; or gather support for a challenging experience or life-altering illness. Exchanging ideas, brainstorming, and obtaining advice are what networking groups are all about, so embrace them.

FREE YOURSELF FROM FEAR

"Everything you've ever wanted is on the other side of fear."

~ George Addair ~

ONE OF the biggest reasons for abandoning our goals, or worse, for not setting ourselves any targets to begin with, is the fear of failing. It took me a long time to stop my inner demons from taking over, and yet I still occasionally struggle with self-doubt, anxiety, and fear even though I have all the motivational tools I need to keep me moving forward.

It was only after my resolution challenge ended that I began to accept failure in a positive way. When I set this challenge, I had every intention of driving myself towards the finish line as hard as I could, but eventually, life took over and the everyday stuff tripped me up. My sister-in-law refers to these as speed wobbles, which is a phrase I love. I always picture someone tripping over a paving stone as they rush down the street and then trying to turn it into a wave at a fictional person across the road.

I've had hundreds of speed wobbles, but each time it's taught me something new—something I've been able to use on different projects or in alternative situations. Don't fear the speed wobble—just turn it into a wave.

When I didn't complete a task or had a bad week on my resolution challenge, I blogged about it. At first, this was difficult, like I was admitting defeat, but the number of comments I received on these types of posts outweighed those on the achievement articles. Everyone could relate to feeling like a failure or wanting to pack it all in and forget you ever started. I realised at that point how important it was to be totally honest about my challenge and embrace the fact that I was, in fact, a woman with hopes and dreams, tapping away at her laptop from the kitchen table. Hundreds of people across the world understood how I felt, why I felt that way, and were happy to share their experiences and encouragement. When I had a bad day, those comments on my blog and messages on social media spurred me on. Those guys became my cheerleading squad members.

One of my best friends, Nikki, always tells me how much better she feels knowing I'm having a bad day. It's said in the nicest possible way, and we laugh because I know what she means. She once told me that I was her poster girl. She sees my online brand as a success. To her, I'm a productive author and blogger, publishing content and visiting fairs, running workshops or preparing talks, and she often told me how seeing my online posts and busy schedule made her worry that she wasn't doing enough of the same for her own business and life. We've talked about this at length, and I was happy to admit that the constant need to have an online presence was overwhelming some days. She could then see my "busy" life for what it was—no time for fun, and always having to come across as upbeat, inspiring, and happy. Life isn't always like that, and so we discussed how I should open up more and share the negative days as well as the positive. That piece of advice not only made Nikki feel better, knowing there was a *real me* behind the success, but also gave me the confidence to share posts about burning the dinner, laddering my tights, or not meeting a deadline. It helped me to be more authentic, and I learned how to walk away and take a break when it got too much.

When I'm feeling swamped and need to vent, Nikki is always there with sound advice. We meet up for coffee, and she'll giggle and tell me how she's thankful that my bad day has made her feel ten times better about her own procrastination. Nikki is a valuable member of my cheerleading squad, as she's honest and supportive. We appreciate one another and laugh at our failures, learn from each other's goals, and make sure to lift the other up when necessary. I know exactly how she feels, though, as I've watched other entrepreneurs online and wondered how the hell they can look so sleek, host sell-out workshops, and still have time to post a selfie from a woodland trail with their 2.4 children and the family dog.

We are all guilty of comparing ourselves to others, of nourishing our fear that we aren't good enough, or that we aren't as good as X, Y, or Z, but this guilt is in varying degrees of intensity. I've often wished that I could live in a warm country like my hugely successful cousin, Becky. Or that I drove a super sexy Land Rover Evoque like my friend, Liz. These are the kind of comparisons that are fleeting thoughts rather than a crippling destruction of our self-esteem. I love these thoughts because they shape our ambitions. They motivate us to want to earn enough to buy a lovely car and travel to interesting places.

At the start of the year I bought a couple of life planners to help me plot out my world domination. As a stationery geek, this was no hardship, and as I've mentioned in an earlier chapter, planning helps me achieve success because everything is written down for me to keep track of.

At the same time, I joined some Facebook groups dedicated to boosting our inspiration, motivating us to achieve our goals, and empowering us to succeed—all the things that I value in my life and strive to pass on to others. The fit was perfect, and I became as active as time allowed in these groups.

Roll the clock forward a few months, and I started to feel twitchy about some of the groups I had joined. Don't get me wrong; there is absolutely nothing wrong with blowing your own trumpet. I've posted about my own success on more than one occasion. If we don't share our achievements, especially if you run an online business, then nobody will know you exist.

It took a fair amount of soul-searching before I realised that it wasn't the groups that had changed—it was me. My inner monologue of destruction was reading the "look at what I've launched/sold/done" as a way to prove that I wasn't there yet, wherever *there* may be. Perhaps I was being overly sensitive, or in need of rereading my Cognitive Behaviour Therapy (CBT) notes, but the feel of those groups had shifted for me.

Instead of feeling motivated, I felt drained. Instead of being inspired to achieve, I felt useless and defeated. I knew that my depression had something to do with this; the cognitive settings in my brain were overloading with the "I'm not good enough" chatter. So, what did I do?

I backed away from the groups. Some of them I left, which meant that the notifications no longer appeared in my feed, and others I stopped interacting with, so the algorithms did their job and buried the posts until I might need them again. I felt better immediately.

It came as a surprise to me how intensely I began comparing myself to these other women and how I judged my own self-worth because of their achievements. I was so sure that being a part of those communities would be the best thing for my personal development, and yet it backfired, leaving me feeling empty.

Comparing yourself to others can be the root of self-doubt and fear, and it can be dangerous. We are unique in every way, and we should acknowledge this fact. I worry about my daughter who, at fifteen, can be influenced by the celebrities she loves and the body image that is portrayed on the cover of every magazine.

Surrounding ourselves (online or in real life) with people who support us is important. Understanding how much damage comparing ourselves to others can do is the first step in correcting these thoughts and releasing those fears.

Does this resonate with you? Perhaps you find yourself comparing your life to just one person or a set of friends. What could you do to correct this?

Here are a few ideas that I've come up with to help:

- Be kinder to yourself—Notice the negative talk and release those thoughts.
- Write it down—I've mentioned my love of journaling before, but I can't stress enough the benefits of writing down what you are grateful for or using a happiness jar.
- Focus on what *you* have—Cherish your family/home/job and don't direct your attention towards what others have.
- Commit to a self-care plan—Look after your physical, emotional, and spiritual needs every day. Commit to nurturing yourself to be the best version of you.

Fear can hold you back and prevent you from achieving greatness. It's a simple emotion that can thwart everything you do in your daily life. When I was training in Emotional Freedom Therapy (EFT), my tutor taught me a wonderful acronym that I use regularly:

FEAR = False Evidence Appearing Real

Whenever I got worked up about my resolution challenge, or any of my projects or events, I would think about that phrase, and it would calm me down. It's human nature to worry about new circumstances, opportunities, or occasions, but it *is* possible to work through those fears and achieve the success we deserve.

When I wrote my Motivate Me workshops, which I ran over the course of a year at a local conference venue, I chose Facing Fear as my first topic. Running workshops was not a new thing for me, but this was a different, larger venue, where I would stand at the front of a conference room full of expectant faces, instead of sitting around in a group environment sipping tea and chatting.

Anyone who knows me will tell you that I am a talker. My school reports were full of "Shelley would get more done if she stopped talking and concentrated on the task at hand." Talking to family, friends, colleagues, or even a stranger on the bus is entirely different from public speaking.

Starting my workshop schedule off with a talk on fear seemed quite apt, as I was totally freaked out about standing up in front of a crowd of people. In the end, I referred to that acronym, False Evidence Appearing Real, and worked through why I was fearful of doing the talk. I had to recognise that there was no evidence to sustain my worries. The audience wasn't going to flay me. They were successful women who had paid to hear me talk—I shouldn't fear them; I should thank them. Turning fear on its head helped me to step out of my comfort zone and present a series of workshops that helped those groups of ladies, and that's something I'm incredibly proud of.

How did I turn fear on its head? I accepted that the audience's participation and reaction were out of my control. That's the biggest fear of all, isn't it? – not being in control. Will they like me? Will they enjoy what I have to say? Will it be useful? And will I say "um" a million times? In the end, I stood up and talked to that group as if I was chatting with friends in my living room. Yes, I said "um." Yes, there were a few questions that I couldn't answer, but I calmly told the audience that I would find the solution and send it to them via email. Yes,

I was nervous, but I knew what I was talking about, and I could share it effectively.

It would have been far too easy to cancel the events, pull a sickie, or never even attempt to expand my business in the first place, but then I would have let fear win. There are loads of things that I could have done to turn fear on its head. I could have taken a public speaking course and learned how to stand, project my voice, and avoid the "umm." I could have collaborated with another workshop facilitator to share the burden. Anything is better than letting fear win and avoiding a situation that has the potential to boost my business.

Can you tell me what you are afraid of? To be able to face your fears you first need to know what they are. Think about classic fears for a moment. What would you add to this list? Dentist, illness, death, being alone, crowds, rejection, failure, losing your job, disapproval.

We deal with our fears constantly. In fact, we deal with a wide variety of fears on a daily basis. Fear of being late for work, fear of not being able to finish a project on time, fear of getting lost if you are driving somewhere new. These are concerns that, while still uncomfortable, wouldn't stop us from doing what was necessary.

I'm hopeless at navigation and need to write out a clear route plan of where I need to be and how long it will take me to get there. It's my way of coping with the fear of getting lost. Of course, I could stay at home and never leave the house nor drive anywhere new. It would certainly prevent my fear and anxiety from surfacing. I've discovered that as long as I'm prepared (map, directions, petrol, packed lunch, and spade), I'll be fine. The addition of a satnav has also reduced my fears considerably.

Let's think about the physical reactions we have to fear. What does our body do in response to a fearful situation? Can you add to the following list? Sweaty palms, palpitations, perspiration, headaches, nausea, migraines, stuttering, butterflies. If you're anything like me, you'll have experienced these sensations at certain times in your life;

they are entirely natural, as it's our body's way of keeping us safe. Way back in caveman days, our ancestors relied on these sensations to stay fed and unharmed. The fight-or-flight reaction helped them to decide if they were in potential danger, which was especially useful when face-to-face with a sabre-toothed tiger.

Have you ever let these sensations stop you from doing something? I nearly didn't attend a writers' conference in London because of my fears. My finger hovered over the "buy ticket" button for so long that I almost got a cramp. As I looked at the screen with the event details, I reread the itinerary and knew, without any doubt, that it would be a hugely beneficial day. But I still paused. My palms were sweaty, my head started to pound, and my stomach was churning. Eventually, I booked the ticket. Why? Because I knew that this conference was a step towards my goals; it would bring me to a network of like-minded people, and it would be a lot of fun. It was. I had the most amazing day, ate my lunch while sitting next to a best-selling author, made a ton of new friends and came home with a notepad bulging at the seams with ideas and notes. I nearly let fear stop me from this experience. That conference was five years ago, and I've been to several more since then, as well as some book/author fairs. I look forward to them now.

You may not believe that it's possible to overcome your fears. You may have set yourself a goal, and now you're going through a stage of "Why did I think I could do this? Why am I bothering?" I hope that by the time you finish this book, you will feel more motivated to achieve your dreams and more confident to face your fears. Living proof of these possibilities surrounds us every day. Just look at the newspaper and read about the bride who was told she would never walk again but who made it up the aisle on her wedding day. Watch your children at sports day as they cross the finish line and glow with achievement. Volunteer for charities such as Women's Aid and meet the incredible women who survived against all the odds.

The way to overcome your fears is to rethink how you look at them. We all have fears, and they're as varied and personal as our goals. Our circumstances are all very different, and our fears are relevant to us—they are unique. Or are they? What if I told you that there is only one fear? Just one. Do you think you could overcome it then?

Fear is simply a belief that we can't handle something, whether that's a situation, an event, or an opportunity. It's this belief that keeps us holding on to our fears. When we face something, we realise that it wasn't as bad as we thought it would be. We *believed* it was going to be an awful thing, but that ended up being false.

Here's an example: if my fifteen-year-old daughter came home and said she was going to bungee jump for charity, my automatic mum reaction would be, "Whoa! That's not a good idea; it's not safe." However, if she was determined, and I found out that it was supervised by teachers, then my second default mum response would be, "Okay, but be careful; it's dangerous." Can you see what I'm doing wrong? I'm projecting my beliefs onto her. I can't handle that she's growing up and wants to do things independently of me.

We all project our fears onto our children, family, and friends, but we don't realise the harm that it's doing because we believe that we are caring, thoughtful, and loving. I can't handle the fact that my children are getting older and will one day be at university, married, and have homes of their own. *I can't handle being on my own* = fear of being alone. I could change this by projecting my fears of a big, bad world onto my children, so they never want to leave home. Of course, this isn't something I would ever do. I love my children, and I want them to explore the world, love, laugh, make mistakes, learn, and appreciate everything they have. They can only do this if I let go of the belief that I can't handle being alone and let them go. They'll come back to me, even if it's only to deliver bags of washing or for a Sunday lunch, but they'll return with passion in their soul and a sparkle in their eyes.

Rewording what you say to yourself, your children, and your family and friends can help to release these long-held beliefs and allow you to move forward. Start to develop a trust in your ability to handle whatever comes your way. Put it into perspective. Recite the acronym "False Evidence Appearing Real." Understand that you are in control of your beliefs and, subsequently, your fears. I've got some tips that might help you to begin reducing your fears:

Build your confidence—Once I had been to that writers' conference, my fear disappeared. I knew that I could handle that type of situation again and that I would enjoy it. Even though I felt nervous each time I attended an event, my confidence grew, and I was better equipped emotionally to handle it. Don't confuse nerves with fear.

Just do it—Doing that one thing that scares you the most can open up new opportunities and experiences. It doesn't have to be a huge thing, such as speaking in public or running a marathon. It could be joining a slimming group or doing a zip wire. Go out and do it.

Realise that you're not on your own—Fear can make us think that we are in this alone. Nobody could understand how you're feeling, right? Wrong. Following my writers' conference, I wrote a blog post about the benefits of the event, and I added a small paragraph about how frightened I'd been before the day. I received an influx of comments from people all over the world following a similar theme: "I felt like that when I went to..." and "That's exactly how I felt when I did..." You may be the one experiencing fear when you do something new, but so is everyone else.

Forget the "what ifs"—We live in fear every day, and there are many times when those fears can be so great that they consume us. Fear of illness or the death of a loved one can be overwhelming. We have NO control over the "what ifs" in life, but we can't put our lives on hold "just in case," so we have to learn to live in harmony with them.

When my cousin passed away from SUDEP (Sudden Unexplained Death from Epilepsy) just before his twenty-fifth birthday,

I remember wondering whether, if my aunt had known his condition could be fatal, she would she have allowed her son to live the full, exciting life he led. Or would she have wrapped him in cotton wool? None of us knew that epilepsy could be fatal, and we all feel the hole that losing Lee left behind, but he achieved more in his twenty-four years than some people do in eighty or ninety years. He never let fear of his condition hold him back, and his legacy will live on forever through his charity: www.leessmile.co.uk.

The most powerful tool to reduce your fear is to *believe in yourself.* Easier said than done, I hear you say, but if you can stop feeding yourself negative thoughts, you're halfway there. I've suffered from self-doubt for more years than I care to remember. That little voice in my head will scream my insecurities back at me if I dare to show any gumption. When I started posting on my blog, and when my first book was published, I was overwhelmed with insecurity. Not only was I putting myself out there for the world to see by pouring out my inner thoughts, actions, and dreams, but I was on a social platform that actively requested honest feedback. Book reviews on retailer sites or review sites such as Goodreads are the perfect way to thank an author for writing a book, but likewise, those readers who didn't like your book can voice their opinion, and let's not forget that it also gives trolls a platform from which to attack. All my favourite authors have received negative reviews and lived to tell the tale, but when you suffer from self-doubt, every negative comment can feel like the stab of a blade in the gut. Remember when I mentioned there being only one fear—a belief that you can't handle something? Well, reviews are out of my hands. I can't control what people think and say; I have no control over whether or not you, my dear reader, enjoy this book. All of this equates to the fact that I can't handle failure. Who can relate to that feeling?

In the beginning, I took every comment as fact. I could have allowed my fear of failure to overrule my common sense, but I love writing, and more importantly, I love sharing my story so that these experiences can help others, so why should I let my fears control my actions? Remember how we talked about finding something you are passionate about—that one thing you *WANT* more than anything? For me, it's to be a writer. I'm living my dream at the moment, but if I allowed my fear and insecurities to win, my dream would crumble around me. I, therefore, acknowledged any negative comments and took on board the feedback. They made me face my self-doubt head-on, and I realised that each review had been a lesson in my personal development. Now, you might not have to cope with such a public situation to come face-to-face with your anxieties, but I would urge you to take a step back and see what lesson you can take from any situation. Don't give up on your dreams because you don't think you're capable. You *are* more than able, and you *can* overcome these feelings.

To help overcome self-doubt, I use the following tips:

- Surround yourself with positive people—I mentioned earlier how easy it is to project your fears onto the people around you. It's worth noting that our habits, good and bad, are also communicable, and if you surround yourself with negative vibes or bad habits, you are at risk of infecting yourself and losing all ability to move forward with your dreams. Stick with your cheerleading squad.
- Share your knowledge—I've found this to be a huge boost for my self-esteem as well as any doubts I have about my abilities. Mentoring, or holding workshops about subjects you know well rekindles your confidence. Think back to when you told someone about your job, your passion, or a product you love. Your voice changes, your eyes sparkle, and you spread pleasant vibes.
- Go back to school—Not in the scary, rewind the clock to the sixteen-year-old you way, but in an evolving your

skill base way. Take classes and read how-to books on the subjects that matter to you. Expanding your knowledge will reduce your self-doubt and fears and raise your confidence.

- Accept that it's okay to fail—I believe this was one of the most valuable lessons that I took away from my resolution challenge. It's *okay* to fail. Rejections are part of life, but it is how you deal with them that matters. Think about J. K. Rowling for a minute. Her Harry Potter manuscript was rejected by twelve different publishers before Barry Cunningham picked it up while at Bloomsbury. Embrace those setbacks and learn from them.

There's a fabulous exercise that shows us the power of our inner dialogue and how being of a negative frame of mind can have an impact on everything we do. I'd love for you to have a go at this; share it with your family and friends, especially kids or young adults, as they'll learn a lot from it. You'll need two people:

Person number one—Stand up and lift your arms out to the sides to shoulder height and bunch your hands into fists. Now muster all your strength to stop person number two from pushing your arms back down to your sides.

Person number two—Place your hands on the top of person number one's arms and try to push them down. You'll find it difficult to do because they are concentrating on being strong.

Person number one—Now close your eyes and repeat ten times (either out loud or in your head) "I am a weak and unworthy person." Open your eyes and repeat the steps above.

Person number two—You'll find it easy to push their arms down this time.

Person number one—Now close your eyes and repeat ten times (either out loud or in your head) "I am a strong and worthy person." Open your eyes and repeat the first steps.

Person number two—You'll find it hard to push their arms down this time.

STOP feeding yourself those negative thoughts!

"The thing you fear most has no power. Your fear of it is what has the power. Facing the truth really will set you free."

~ Oprah Winfrey ~

DE-STRESS FOR SUCCESS

Before I move on to the next chapter, I wanted to share a small section about stress and how to combat it. Along with fear, stress can cause us to abandon our goals or prevent us from achieving our desires.

It's worth pointing out that we can have good and bad stress in our lives. Good stress is the kind that helps us to excel at sports or stand up in front of a room full of people and deliver a presentation. It makes us slightly uncomfortable, but it doesn't stop us from moving forward.

Bad stress, on the other hand, can change our behaviours, reduce our creativity and productivity, and also cause us long-term damage: physically, emotionally, and spiritually. Life can be demanding enough without pushing ourselves to achieve goals, but how else are we going to excel at life, seize new opportunities, or create exciting avenues to explore? Learning to get stressful situations under control is a great way to leave yourself free to enjoy your life and career and accept all the wonderful things that are coming your way.

First of all, it helps to understand what stress is and how it affects us, then we can figure out the most efficient plan of action for de-stressing. We all have our way of dealing with stuff. Some people thrive on a higher level of stress than others. A friend and client of mine, Ann, always astounded me when she talked about her job. She never sat still for longer than two minutes, rushing from meeting to meeting, planning and executing huge road shows, and managing a team of workers. I was exhausted just listening to her, but she loved it, and she glowed when talking about her daily role, and that's how we differ. If I were in that type of career, I would burn out before the end of the first week. Give me ten sets of feet and my reflexology couch over that any day.

If you are feeling stressed, be it with your job, health, friendships, or your goals, you will probably experience racing thoughts and be exceptionally irritable. I know that I can get quite snappy when I'm stressed, which isn't fair to anyone who happens to be in my vicinity. If you are a fan of personal development, you will have heard the phrase "fight-or-flight" on a regular basis. If you haven't heard of this, I'll give you a quick overview.

Stress causes your nervous system to release a surge of hormones, including adrenaline and cortisol, into your body, which is called the fight-or-flight response. It prepares you for an emergency, and it's our body's way of keeping us safe from threats.

Your heart pounds faster, muscles tighten, blood pressure rises, your breath quickens, and your senses become sharper. These physical changes increase your strength and stamina—we've all heard about incredible feats of strength with people lifting objects such as a car to rescue someone. This is the adrenaline and cortisol flooding the system. In the past it would have saved the lives of our ancestors. That rush of hormones prompts us either to fight to secure our dinner or protect our family, or to run away, which is always helpful when up against a ferocious predator. These days, the wild man-eating predators of yesteryear are gone. Instead, their replacements are more often dressed in a suit, and called bosses.

The surge of hormones will usually return to normal once the predator (boss) has gone away and you feel safe again. However, if that stress is a constant in your life—for example, in the event of abuse or a highly stressful career—the hormones remain in your system and lead to a host of nasty symptoms. The body doesn't know the difference between a physical threat and a psychological one. It doesn't care if you've had an argument with your partner or been threatened at knifepoint by a mugger—it will react in the same way. Therefore, if you are always worried about something, your stress levels will be permanently switched on.

Recognising when your stress levels are high is important, as stress can sneak up on us very fast. You begin to think it's fairly typical, adapt to accommodate these new changes, and then refrain from noticing how it's affecting you and your life.

Stress also affects our mind, our body, and our behaviour. I've added a few examples below that are fairly common warning signs that you can watch out for.

- Memory problems
- Being overly negative
- Anxious thoughts
- Moodiness and irritability
- Not being able to relax
- Feeling isolated and alone
- Eating too much/too little
- Procrastinating
- Nervous habits, such as nail biting

- Loss of sex drive
- Diarrhoea/Constipation
- Aches and pains
- Frequent colds

This is by no means an exhaustive list, but it's worth looking out for any signs as you work towards achieving success. We want to complete our tasks and claim a victory over our resolutions and goals, but pushing ourselves beyond the limits isn't worth it. I read an interesting article about Andrew Sullivan, a prolific writer and super-blogger. From working so hard and becoming obsessed with blogging, the web, statistics, and his smartphone, he became seriously ill, contracting four bronchial infections in twelve months. The signs were there, but he didn't heed the warnings until it was too late. Andrew now tries to include meditation in his routine to try to counter the negative effects of the digital age that threaten to swamp us all.

If you do begin to notice any symptoms sneaking into your daily life, take a step back and ask yourself a few questions.

Is it work, home, family, friends, or environment related?

When I first opened my holistic health business, I would worry about not getting enough clients. Seven years later I'm worried about not having enough hours in the day to help everyone. Our stresses change over time, so it's vital to stay mindful. If you are setting yourself a goal to write a book, then you might worry about people not wanting to read your work; if you want to start your own business, you might stress over the bills, employees, or marketing. Remain conscious of your thoughts and your fears. As we discussed earlier, there are many techniques to help you overcome fears, and there are loads of ways to cope with stress. Look back over the Self-Care Plan section. All of those techniques work well for de-stressing and are worth adding to your personal development magic box.

Start a weekend ritual to help keep stress at bay. Use the ideas in the self-care plan, or come up with your own. Here's an example of how you can look after your mental, emotional, and physical health in short bursts every weekend. Add them to your weekly intentions list and try to make time to do them. Stress is not something you want to invite into your life, so finding a happy balance is imperative. When I did my resolution challenge, I was able to de-stress by firstly breaking down my main goal into minuscule, manageable chunks, assigning specific days/times to action my goals, and pre-planning. Incorporating the self-care elements into my routine was common sense and helped me to remain focused. By doing this I was able to succeed in completing the yearlong challenge, but it also set me up to achieve my ultimate dream of seeing my first book in print.

Start and finish the weekend feeling de-stressed and ready for action.

Friday night

- Ditch the takeaway and opt for wholesome foods.
- Jump in a bubble bath and soak up the relaxation for half an hour.
- Meditate for ten minutes before bed.

Saturday

- Enjoy a great breakfast.
- Get outside and experience nature.
- Do something that makes you smile, such as going to the theatre/cinema.

Sunday

- Meet a friend for a coffee.

- Enjoy a homemade spa with exfoliating scrubs, oils, and smelly candles.
- Do a spot of decluttering.

Generating a few simple changes can make a huge difference, and you'll be amazed how it makes you feel.

REAL WOMEN, REAL LIVES

ONE OF the features that I run on my motivational blog is "Real Women, Real Lives." We are surrounded by inspirational women on a daily basis; they are on the television, the radio, or they've written the books we buy or the articles/blog posts we read. It's easy to put a celebrity on a pedestal and desire their lifestyle, power, and determination. However, we don't need to turn to the glossy magazines or the big screen to find inspirational women who can motivate us to succeed—they live next door, work alongside us, and talk to us at the supermarket.

I wanted to include some of these incredible ladies in this book. These women have succeeded on their chosen path or turned misfortune into positivity. They have conquered illness or gone above and beyond to help others and make a difference. They are your friends, co-workers, and neighbours. I was honoured that some of these remarkable women agreed to share their stories with us, revealing their motivational journey and the vision behind their success.

Hopefully, you'll be able to take a little inspiration from their stories and turn this positivity into a way of motivating yourself to achieve something important to you, whether that's to write a book, lose weight, or start a charity campaign; the vision and determination possessed by these women can't fail to move you.

FINDING YOUR CREATIVE GOALS WITH AUTHOR TERRY TYLER

Terry Tyler lives in the North of England with her husband. She is a well-known author with over thirteen titles. She is an active Twitter user and uses her networking skills to help promote fellow authors and bloggers. Her contemporary women's fiction includes romance and suspense but can also be a little edgy and a bit dark on occasion. They are always about real life, covering meaningful topics that we face every day.

I asked Terry a few questions about her creative journey. Here's what she had to say:

Q. What motivated you to write and publish your first book?

A. I actually wrote several novels in the 1990s, before self-publishing via existed; I wasn't working at the time and just thought that I'd see if I could write one. Then life got in the way, and I stopped. In 2009 I met my husband, who read one of my manuscripts and encouraged me to start again. It was hard to get into the swing of it, like wading through treacle in cement boots, at first! But I knew that I'd hate myself if I gave up. When *You Wish* was more or less finished, I sent it out in instalments to friends to see what they thought. Luckily, the response was very positive (i.e. they kept saying "hurry up and write the next bit"). Then I heard about ebook publishing—and the rest is you-know-what!

Q. What writing-related goals do you set for yourself?

A. To publish two books a year. So far I've kept to that—and exceeded it in 2013!

Q. Are you able to self-motivate, and if so, how do you keep yourself writing on a regular basis?

A. I'm lucky in that yes, I am able to self-motivate—I think it also depends how much you want to do it (and it helps that I've been self-employed too). Perhaps the answer is this: if you're finding it hard to sit down and write, or paint, or if you're trying to lose weight or give up smoking, perhaps what you're trying to do is not quite the right fit, or it's not the right time—things may change in six months! I say this because I recently had three ideas for my next book and was dillydallying; I couldn't make my mind up or get going with any of them. Then, only yesterday, another idea popped into my head, which I know is THE ONE—and I can't wait to get started. When I really love and believe in what I'm doing, I want to write whenever I can; so that's the answer, I think.

Here's a comparison between creativity and life in general: you know when you're going out with some guy that you're not *that* keen on, but you try to persuade yourself that you are? So you think "Maybe I just don't want a relationship right now." But then another man comes along—the one who totally hits the spot—and suddenly you most definitely *do* want a relationship, after all! I think creativity is a bit like that. If you don't love it, it may not be right for you.

Q. Tell us about a time when you felt demoralised over your creativity. How did you raise your spirits?

A. I think all writers go through phases of thinking that they're rubbish. When that happens to me, I just stop. I read, escape into a Netflix series, or do something domestic or anything else that is useful/productive. Inevitably, a couple of days later, a new review or a lovely message from a reader will appear that will make me think "Hey, perhaps I'm not so bad after all!" Or I'll just wake up in a better mood. Sometimes waiting for that better mood is all you can do.

Q. What advice would you give to someone who wants to write their first book?

A. First, make sure you really do want to (see earlier question!)—in which case you may have already made tentative steps. If lack of self-confidence is a problem, or if you've never written anything before, try a short story first, or even just small passages or essays. Then show them to someone who you can trust to give you an honest answer without being too brutal! Don't expect too much of yourself at first; don't expect the first novel you write even to be publishable, necessarily. Most successful writers have a ton of unpublished stuff tucked away. Read articles on the web about mistakes often made by first-time authors (I've written a couple!). Don't think in terms of book sales; write from the heart. I can recommend an excellent book that might help if you think you have the talent but don't know how to bring it out—*Back to Creative Writing School* by Bridget Whelan.

Terry not only achieves her goal of writing two books a year, but she is also a member of a book review team (read her reviews at www.terrytylerbookreviews.blogspot.co.uk). You can also find her blogging at www.terrytyler59.blogspot.co.uk where she encourages her readers to share stories about relationships, nostalgia, TV, and a host of other topics.

MAINTAINING WEIGHT LOSS WITH JULIE KIRBY, SLIMMING WORLD CONSULTANT

Julie Kirby lives in the West Midlands with her husband and daughter and works as a Slimming World consultant.

I met Julie just over two years ago and found her to be an absolute ray of sunshine, inspirational, and a wonderful support. No matter where her group members are on their weight-loss journey, Julie can help them achieve their ultimate goal. Anyone who has struggled with their weight will understand how it can consume your every thought. Joining a slimming group not only gives you the tools to start a healthy-eating regime, it provides you with a ready-made support network—and great friends!

I asked Julie about her weight-loss journey. Here's what she said:

Q. What motivated you to join Slimming World?

A. It was a dear friend of mine, Yvonne, who suggested that we join a local Slimming World group. She has since lost five stone in weight and now runs her own group.

Q. Tell us about a hurdle that got in the way of your weight loss. How did you go about overcoming it?

A. Chocolate! It's always chocolate that proves to be a hurdle. It's far too lovely and a great comfort food—the fact that it's so easily available doesn't help! I overcome this by allowing myself a Curly Wurly and adding it to my daily Syn total. I also found it difficult to plan family meals around long working hours because my husband and daughter weren't on the plan. They have since embraced the healthy meals, and I can now make a Slimming World recipe that everyone will enjoy.

Q. Did you ever feel like your weight-loss goal was hopeless? Why did you keep on going? Who/What inspired you to succeed?

A. Yes, I did feel like my weight loss wasn't going where I wanted it to be on occasion. I found that staying to the group meetings was hugely inspiring, as I discovered many tips and new recipes from fellow members that kept me going. My consultant was a huge encouragement too as were my friends who supported me week in and week out. Reading the success stories in the Slimming World magazine is another brilliant way to feel motivated.

Q. As a Slimming World consultant, how do you motivate a member who is struggling?

A. I take them back to the beginning and remind them of why they are doing the plan. There is a reason that member joined, be it a special event, a health issue, or a desire to live a healthier lifestyle. Sometimes we need to recap why we started on our weight-loss journey.

Q. What advice would you give to someone who wants to join a slimming group?

A. If someone wants to join my Slimming World group, I tell them that it's the best plan I have ever done—and it works! Getting to my goal weight was the best I've ever felt—not just in health but in confidence. I wish I'd done it sooner.

To find out where your nearest Slimming World group is, enter your postcode into the website: www.slimmingworld.co.uk

SURVIVING AGAINST THE ODDS WITH HEATHER VON ST. JAMES

For many of us, February is a cold and miserable month that must be suffered through to reach the bounty of spring that follows; however, February is marked on Heather's calendar every year as an exceptional month.

Heather Von St. James was given just fifteen months to live back in 2005. She was diagnosed with pleural mesothelioma, a form of cancer that cost Heather her left lung. At the age of thirty-six and only three months after giving birth to her beautiful daughter, Lily Rose, she received the life-altering diagnosis.

"I had malignant pleural mesothelioma. The blank look on my face told him that I had no idea what I was up against…

…The doctor asked me if my dad was a miner or if he had ever worked with asbestos. I saw myself as a child, wearing my father's work jacket, white and crusty from drywall dust. The cancer was in the lining of my left lung."

Faced with surgery, Heather tried to wrap her head around the fact that she had cancer. She encountered an uncertain future and the possibility that she might never see her daughter grow up. Everything she read confirmed what the doctors had been telling her; she would be dead in fifteen months.

Brushing aside the tears and loss of control, Heather was able to take command of her fear, reciting one of my favourite acronyms: FEAR—False Evidence Appearing Real.

"If you take a long hard look at fear, that is exactly what it is. It builds up to eclipse every rational thought, and when it comes time to face those fears, you realise that they are not what you thought.

When I faced my fears, I found out I was stronger than I ever imagined."

Heather encourages people to face their fears. She still has concerns that her cancer may return, or that her husband or daughter may get sick, but she doesn't let these fears control her.

There is a beautiful website where Heather shares her story in the hope that her journey will help others who are coping with the same symptoms and frightening experience. The site tracks her incredible story from the fear and denial, through the treatment, loss, and setbacks, and eventually to survivorship. It is a brave and insightful story, and I urge everyone to read her story—"Beating the Odds."

www.mesothelioma.com/heather/survivor/#intro

February 2016 marked a special anniversary for Heather as she reached the incredible milestone of being a ten-year mesothelioma cancer survivor. It is her aim to raise awareness about mesothelioma, a deadly cancer caused by exposure to asbestos.

On average, the three thousand people who are diagnosed with mesothelioma every year are given ten months to live. That's just three hundred days!

For more information on mesothelioma cancer, please visit the Mesothelioma Cancer Alliance at www.mesothelioma.com

You can also follow Heather on Facebook and Twitter:

www.twitter.com/HeatherVSJ

www.facebook.com/HeatherVonStJames

"When hope is in the equation, the odds don't matter." I truly believe that, and I plan on being around for many more years to come.

~ Heather Von St. James ~

MOTIVATE ME!

AS THE title of this book points out, motivation can help us achieve success in everything we do. But what if, occasionally, we lose our way or life sends us on a detour? Reminding ourselves of what motivation means can get us back on track and help us to flourish in life, love, and finding happiness.

Even before I set my resolution challenge or started writing books, I was fascinated by psychology. Training in holistic health was another way to take a peep into people's minds and discover who they were and why they did what they did or why they responded in a particular way. Studying motivation came with the territory. I wanted to help as many people as I could to be the best version of themselves. That often meant that I had to find a way to inspire my clients or motivate them to try a new treatment, or even change their negative thought patterns into positive ones. I read so many books and articles on the topic and also tried out as many techniques as I could in the hope that something would click for me, and I could pass it on to my ladies. The way I see it, motivation falls into three stages, and I like to call it the D.A.D effect.

D = Decision. Without the initial decision to try something new or set a challenge, you can't accomplish anything.

The decision process is important, and that's why planning, organising, and brainstorming are so vital when setting goals or resolutions.

A = Action. You've made the decision to try something new, such as starting your own business, writing a book, or losing weight; now you have to persistently work towards that goal. This could mean arranging meetings with a financial advisor, plotting the chapters of your book, or joining a slimming group.

D = Determination. You could even use the word dedication for this section, as without 100 percent dedication to achieving your goals, you'll never find the determination to see them through. Someone who is committed to their task will put in the time and energy; they will spend hours drawing up business plans, study the art of writing, so they can evolve their own skills to write a better book, or become actively involved in their slimming group by helping out or even paying monthly, which confirms their loyalty to the task.

Over the years many psychologists have analysed the why and how of motivation, coming up with various theories including biological and behavioural instincts, such as the need for water when you're thirsty or the desire to keep your house clean.

They also view motivation in two very different ways: extrinsic, which means our motivation comes from outside influences like winning a prize or receiving praise. The other way is intrinsic, which means all our motivation comes from within us—a bit like me writing my blog for personal gratification. When we set our resolutions/goals/challenges, we probably use a mix of both. When I set up my resolution challenge, I knew it was a personal journey with the ultimate aim of writing more (intrinsic motivation), but it was also about producing something worth selling at the end. At the time I didn't know what that was because writing nonfiction books had never been on my to-do list. I did believe, however, that it would give me another avenue to explore within my holistic business, such as running workshops (extrinsic motivation).

When you look at the goals you've set for yourself, think about the influences behind them and make sure they fit into the D.A.D effect for optimum success.

When I began running my Motivate Me workshops, I used to leave a handout on all the chairs for the attendees to take away with them. It was my interpretation of motivation. I'd like to share this with you in the hope that it resonates with what you are planning for yourself.

M = Mindfulness

O = Optimism

T = Trusting in the process

I = Inner wisdom

V = Validation

A = Activating your dreams

T = Thinking outside the box

E = Empowering yourself

M is for being mindful and learning to be in the now. Slowing down and becoming aware of what your mind/body is telling you enables you to discover new opportunities and experiences. Try a five-minute meditation every morning or night.

O is for optimism. Start to look at your life through the eyes of a child, with innocence. See the simple things that can make a profound difference to your day/week/month, such as smiling, holding a door open, or paying someone a compliment. All these acts add to our well of optimism.

T is for trust. I'm not a life coach or a neuroscientist; I'm a single mum who turned her life around when she hit rock bottom. I had to trust that the lessons I'd learned were there for a reason. I believed that the universe could deliver, and more importantly, I began to trust myself that I could survive, make changes, and be the person I wanted to be.

I is for inner wisdom. You have the ability to change bad habits, to find happiness, and to love who you are. Sometimes you may forget that your inner wisdom exists. It's always there, just beneath the surface, and it's ready to provide you with the answers you long for. Using oracle cards can be the perfect way to tap into your inner wisdom.

V is for validation. For every issue you face or problem you think you can't handle, there are a hundred other women/men who have been through this and have come out at the other end. You can use their wisdom and experiences as case studies. Let those who have walked this path before you be mentors, or join a support network or social networking group. These are all ways to validate that you *can* get through anything. Don't be afraid to ask for help when you need it. You are not alone.

A is for activating your dreams. These are the action points that you take to make things happen. By taking that first step, you begin a chain reaction that pulls your dream towards you and activates those wishes into becoming a reality. Without this stage, you become stuck.

T is for thinking outside the box. Learning to change the way you think can have a profound impact on your life. When you are worried about an issue, stop for a moment and put yourself in the shoes of someone you admire—a strong person who never seems to be fazed by anything—what would they do? Come at your problems and fears from an alternative direction.

E is for empowerment. In today's society, you have the opportunity to sign up to be a part of powerful social communities, both online and in real life. A group of friends with similar interests and beliefs can be invaluable. At home, you may be part of a networking group or a slimming club; perhaps you're a member of the Women's Institute, a book club, or a regular coffee morning event. All of these groups empower you. Being around like-minded people, meeting new friends, and sharing that positive energy will feed your motivation to succeed and will grow your desire to be the best you can be.

If we think about our resolutions, goals, or projects as one big jigsaw, then by collecting all the pieces and slotting them together, we achieve success. All the sections of this book are like those jigsaw pieces.

- Setting your goal—the why, what, and how
- Planning your action points
- Organising your life to accommodate your goals
- Making sure you allow yourself some time for self-care, so you are strong
- Freeing yourself from doubts and fears
- Learning how to stay motivated to succeed

Every single piece is important, and if you think you'll achieve your goals faster by skipping a step, then you'll fail. We can't change our lives on willpower alone, even if we think we've got our habits under control, or we are determined to succeed. Life will inevitably take over and throw us a scenario that tests our resolve. I'm pretty proficient when it comes to setting myself a challenge and driving through to the end, but if my heart isn't 100 percent "in it," then I'm just setting myself up for failure.

For example, I gave up drinking alcohol over three years ago, and I haven't touched a drop since because I was determined to become teetotal. I managed to achieve this on pure willpower, not by planning ahead or organising; however, when I took part in my resolution challenge back in 2013, I was a heavy-ish social drinker, and giving up my glasses of chardonnay for a month was sheer torture. At that time in my life, I was happy to have alcohol in my weekly schedule, and so the passion for giving up for my mental and physical health hadn't materialised yet. Going without my Friday glass or three was unthinkable. I did it; I managed to give it up for the month, but I celebrated the end of that thirty-day period with a large glass of rioja.

The only reason that I managed to survive that one month alcohol free was because I'd collected every piece of the jigsaw:

- I set my goal—no alcohol for thirty days.
- I planned accordingly, removing any temptation from the house and adding the challenge to my calendar/diary.
- I organised myself, allocated myself a reward, and was ready to commit to the challenge.

It was tough, but I did it. Now, all these years later, I can't imagine having a glass of wine ever again. We play to our strengths, and we plan for our weaknesses.

CHANGING HABITS

I mentioned being able to get your habits under control earlier. As with willpower, this isn't the easiest thing to do. Anyone who has struggled to give up smoking or lose weight will understand. Our habits can run so deep that changing them is a near impossibility. Or is it?

Think about how easy it is to form a bad habit, such as nail-biting, overeating, or speeding. Before we've had time to think about it, we're a Jaffa Cake-munching nail-biter who drives like Lewis Hamilton. Changing back is where the hard work begins. My eldest son is a nail-biter, and we've tried everything to break his habit. The only thing that works is a distraction technique. When he is fully focused on something, even if it is his Xbox, he doesn't nibble, but if he is sitting aimlessly watching *Friends* reruns, his default action is to bite, bite, bite—another positive reason for switching off the television.

Our habits shape who we are and what we want. Happiness, success, and even body image are all created by our repeated thought patterns. Let's put this into context. We know what we need to do to lose weight—eat less, move more—we've been taught this lesson by our slimming group, our school, our doctor's surgery, and endless nutritional slogans in magazines and on television. Putting this into practice, however, can leave us in a fight to the death with our willpower and habits.

Let's imagine this scenario. You agree to meet a friend at the local coffee shop. It just so happens to be a favourite haunt that serves the best Victoria sponge cake in the area. You are, unfortunately, on yet another healthy-eating regime, but you decide that *this time* being virtuous is going to be a possibility.

Your friend arrives, but they are *not* on a healthy eating regime; in fact, they are celebrating a new job/pay rise/promotion. The friend has arrived at that wonderful ritual where, if and when you succeed in achieving something, you want to celebrate with a reward. That need to reward ourselves is instilled in us from a very early age. I, for one, remember getting a small Playmobil figurine when I had to have a tooth out aged about eight. I was a well-behaved girl and very brave, and so I was rewarded with a gift.

Your friend orders their coffee and a large slice of Victoria sponge cake. What do you do? It is important to understand that at this point your brain will go into automatic mode and dig around for a suitable habit to fill the need you are presenting it with. Do I, or don't I? It remembers that the last time you were in this environment you were emotional, and the cake helped. That was your reward, and so your brain deemed this was worth remembering and presents you with this as your best option.

Your willpower ran off screaming when you walked through the coffee shop door, so all you have left is your habit. "Latte and a slice of Victoria sponge cake, please."

The coffee shop pattern is part of who you are. It's ingrained so deeply that no amount of effort can override it. It's like we are preprogrammed machines destined to repeat the same patterns over and over.

It's probably worth noting that some habits are beneficial for us, and these are the ones we want to encourage, such as brushing your teeth, drinking three litres of water every day or embarking on a healthy-eating plan/daily fitness regime. Good habits also mean that we do worthy things on autopilot because there is nothing new to learn. Our bad habits, on the other hand, mean that we are making the same mistakes over and over.

Believe it or not, it's relatively easy to overcome the pattern of a bad habit. All you have to do is mix up your daily routine a little—do things differently, *or* do different things, and I don't mean in a "resolution challenge fifty-two tasks a year" kind of way. You can rethink everyday simple tasks so that your mind is constantly on alert and working things through—and *not* reverting to habitual thinking.

When I used this technique on myself, it was to try to release some of the habitual self-doubt actions that have thwarted me in the past. I used to get so far with a project and then feel that trickle of fear in my stomach. As soon as it began, I knew I had two choices—carry on, work through it, and succeed, or revert to the safe and comfortable zone where I never achieved anything. If I was going to complete a full year of trials, then I needed to rethink my actions. The *do something different* technique worked so well that I have since adopted it for various other areas of my life, including weight loss, business goals, and relationships.

I've already mentioned how I now opt to turn the television off and make better use of my time. That simple action is pretty much at the core of *doing something different*. Flopping on the sofa night after night to watch *Friends* reruns is a bad habit. As part of my resolution challenge, I went a full seven days without the TV or radio. I didn't miss the hundreds of channels at all; I *did*, however, miss having music in my life. So, by the end of that month, I'd formed a new habit of using my evenings to write my book, and I didn't bother going back to watching reruns. The radio, however, went straight back on, as a life without music is no life at all. You don't have to give up watching telly for that long if you don't want to, but I challenge you to give it up for a full day and night and see what a difference it makes to your routine.

There are so many simple changes you can make to break those bad habits. Doing something different every single day can help you gain plenty of free time, as well as rewire your brain to release those nasty habits that are holding you back.

What could you do differently? How about buying an alternative magazine to the one you usually pick up? What if you tried something new on the menu at your favourite restaurant instead of opting for the same "safe" dish? Try a different exercise class, read a crime novel instead of a romance, go to a different supermarket for your weekly shopping, or go to the cinema or theatre on your own. You might flinch at that last one—who would go to the cinema on their own? Well, I do! It's one of the changes I made to my life that proved to be quite cathartic. At first, I thought it was a bit odd. The cinema was always a fun family event for us, but when I went along for that first time on my own, I discovered a multitude of other solo viewers, hoarding an entire tub of popcorn to themselves and laughing along with everyone else. Nobody batted an eye that I was sitting on my own, and after the first thirty seconds, I felt quite at home and settled down to watch the film. I now book myself in for regular cinema treats as and when I can because I know this is hugely beneficial for me. It ended up being a good habit. Not only do I get to see some great films, but it also helped to boost my confidence and taught me how to be comfortable in my own company.

Here are a few other things you could do differently: go to bed at 10:00 p.m. instead of 11:00 p.m., talk to someone new at work/school, switch off your mobile phone for a full day (eek!), wear flat shoes instead of heels (or vice versa), sing in the shower, take a different route to work/school—the list is endless. Jot a few suggestions in your notebook and try to include them in your daily action plan.

The reason this technique worked so well for me came down to one thing: it showed me how to evaluate everything I did on a daily basis and work out whether or not the things I was doing were worth the effort of doing them. Had I let bad habits take over my life? Yes, quite a few times, but using these exercises allowed me the space to see how I could make changes and implement them. At one point I was spending over an hour on the computer, checking emails and social media, and only half an hour chatting with my kids over dinner—it was then that I realised something had to change.

Be fearless with yourself and attack those bad habits head-on; mix them up with new ideas and different approaches. Be adventurous, spontaneous, and have fun thinking up alternative ways of doing something. Write it all down in your notebook, record what you did and how you felt before and after, and don't let your habits prevent you from achieving success ever again.

WHAT OR WHO MOTIVATES YOU?

We talked about having a cheerleading squad in an earlier chapter, but this time I want you to think about what, or who, motivates you on a deeper level on a daily basis.

When I get asked in interviews what kept me motivated during my yearlong resolution challenge, I always say my kids because they did and continue to do so every day. They stood behind me as I typed up the last hundred words on my fifty thousand-word novel challenge; they were cheering me on when I stepped off the platform and jumped into the abyss on the zip-wire test; and they were the first to tell me how proud they were when I published my first book.

Keeping up with your resolutions or goals is hard enough, but without something, or someone, to keep you motivated, it's far too easy to let your dream fizzle out or leave your successes to go undiscovered. You might know instantly what your motivation is; you may have a partner, parent, or child who inspires you to succeed, or maybe an event, cause, or reason to achieve your goals—a wedding to slim down for, a charity event to spur you on, or a supportive husband/wife who believes in you. Give it some thought, as discovering your motivation can help keep you focused on achieving success.

I ran a series of posts on my blog, offering tips on how to stay motivated to succeed in whatever resolution my readers set for themselves. The blog posts were well-received, so I thought I'd share the basic idea with you too. The first top tip was looking at developing a "daily practice."

When I set my goals, I normally do so when I'm in a positive frame of mind, feeling quite calm and balanced, and I'm usually safely cocooned in my happy place. I'll go to bed with a satisfied smile, knowing I've made an important decision—then morning arrives.

Day one...what do I do now? The initial idea might have mellowed slightly, and the original sparkle has made way for reality. If you've experienced this sense of panic after setting your goals, you're not alone. I've set myself many challenges and then freaked out when the sun began to rise on a new day, and I was faced with getting started. To help myself stay focused, I ask myself three questions:

1. Why am I doing this?
2. When am I doing this?
3. What do I need to achieve success?

I'll use "running a marathon" as an example. If this were my goal, I would answer these questions with the following:

1. Why—To boost my health and raise money for my chosen charity.
2. When—Various societies set regular dates for marathons across the UK and worldwide. If I wanted to run the London Marathon, for example, I'd sign up on their website and add the date (usually April time) to my diary and calendar.
3. What—This is where the idea of a "daily practice" comes in.

There are some daily tasks that we could do to focus ourselves fully on the goal of running a marathon. We could take part in a ten-minute daily mindfulness meditation to help us get our heads in the zone to complete a twenty-six-mile run. Writing for five minutes in a journal could also help, as we could record our feelings about doing this challenge and remember the people we are helping if running for a charity. We could also use it as a training diary/record. Another useful daily practice would involve breathing exercises, and of course, a daily run is vital. To run a marathon effectively, you would need to train—lots—and this needs to be done correctly and with the right support, be it a gym buddy, personal trainer, or running coach.

Don't forget that spending a few minutes looking at your vision board would also count as a daily practice. Surrounding yourself with positive images of what you want to achieve helps you to believe it has already happened.

You don't have to do all of the daily practices; you can pick the one that resonates the most with you, but whatever you choose, make sure you stick to it. If you are fully committed to your goal, doing this regular task will become as much of a habit—a good habit—as brushing your teeth.

Daily practices can be tiny achievements. Signing up for a smaller 5K local race is an action step towards your big goal of running a marathon, and going for a half-hour run every day is another step, or jog, in the right direction. Opening your laptop, clicking on "new document" and typing a sentence is the beginning of writing your book. Searching for a local gym and hitting the join button begins a daily practice that opens you up to fun, fitness, and meeting new friends. Focus on one day at a time.

We can use the same three questions to adopt a weekly intention too. If the thought of having a daily practice is too much to handle, then a weekly intention can be more manageable. Ask yourself the same three questions:

> *Why*—Let's assume our goal is to learn something new. Why we want to do this is more often than not a very personal choice. I love going on holiday to Italy, for example, so learning to speak a few sentences of Italian would be highly beneficial. There are numerous adult language courses that I could take. Learning a new skill can also be of benefit to your business or even give you the skills to set up a new venture.

> *When* you learn your new skill will depend on the learning provider. If it's through a local college, then courses generally start in January or September. Distance learning courses or eCourses can begin at any time to suit you and your needs/schedule.
>
> *What* you need to do to achieve success can be figured out by breaking down your goal. If I were going to learn Italian, I'd enrol in a community course and write down the class time and date in my diary or on my calendar. By signing up and paying for the course, I'm committing myself 100 percent to taking that course. Illness or bad weather may thwart me on the odd occasion, but if the intention is there, I'll return week after week.

Actively leaving the house to attend a weekly class takes away all the stress of setting a weekly intention. You booked the course, paid the fee—now turn up and enjoy yourself. Telling your friends and family just how important the class is to you will help keep you focused and also give you that precious two hours a week for yourself—remember our self-care plan?

Thinking about your goals or resolutions weekly really does help to keep them at the forefront of your mind. You'll notice that slimming groups run every week. The same people show up week after week because they have committed to that date/time. They also know that when they arrive, they will receive support towards achieving success, and it then becomes a valuable part of their week. My mum reached her goal weight five years ago, but she still attends the meetings. Why? Because it keeps her motivated to maintain her success.

If you have several challenges on the go at once, you might find it helpful to use a weekly intention list (I do love my lists). You can split your weekly action points into sections, such as Personal, Business, Kids, and Money. Here's a mix from my personal and business list as an example:

- Book an acupuncture appointment for Friday.
- Buy my brother's birthday present before the end of January.
- Complete the next chapter of my work in progress by the end of February.
- Go over my vision board workshop presentation for next week's course.
- Schedule the next three months' blog posts.

These were my weekly intentions for home and work, and they ran alongside my resolution challenge action points. My advice, when writing your weekly intentions, is to keep it simple. Don't use it as a to-do list. My to-do list has *all* the jobs I need to complete, which includes tasks for home, work, kids, writing, business, social media, and leisure—it covers two A4 sides. If that were my weekly list, then I'd be deep breathing into a paper bag by now. I transfer the items I need to do in that week and include an action point that drives my goal forward—completing the next chapter of my work in progress was my big goal.

It might be worth mentioning at this point that I don't use these techniques all the time. If I did, I'd be doing nothing but list writing, planning, and organising, and wouldn't have any time left to get on with the challenge itself. Use them if you like the sound of them; dismiss them if the exercises are not resonating with you. As I mentioned at the beginning of this book, I'm sharing *everything* I did, and do, in the hope that something will click for you and help you to achieve that success.

One of my regular blog readers, Julia, made a valid observation. She said, "*The more I look into goal setting and intentions, the more I real-*

ise that, for me, long-term aims are more of a hindrance than a help. They encourage me to focus too much on the future and not enough on the present. For now, I'm concentrating on what I want to do today, and more specifically, this morning, this afternoon, this evening." I loved her response and thought it was important to add her comment. If you're feeling a bit overwhelmed about your goals, the planning, or the action steps, it can be disastrous for your motivation—remember how we talked about habits and willpower? If you want to take your goals and break them into daily tasks: a morning, afternoon, and evening task, then do this. It's important to find the right pace and structure to fit your needs if you want to achieve anything. Motivation comes in many shapes, sizes, and structures, so explore them all until you find the right one.

As a summary, I wanted to give you my favourite tips for staying motivated. Call them additional self-care bonuses or just basic guidelines. However you treat them, I think they are a useful addition to the motivational toolbox.

Use a brain dump diary. If your mind is whirling with ideas, thoughts, plans, and your to-do list, write it all down. Before bed, note every thought and feeling you have about your goal—great help for insomnia too.

Schedule a mid-month treat. Coffee with a friend is perfect, as you can support one another and offer advice or inspiration when it's needed.

Get some fresh air. A fifteen-minute walk can reboot the brain and awaken your muscles. The benefits of walking and getting outside are well-documented. Inspiration can strike at any time, but when you are living in the moment, enjoying nature, and boosting your happy hormones, then you are more likely to uncover the answers you are searching for. Make a date in your diary to have a "fresh air Friday." Add it to your weekly intention list.

Allocate some pamper time. Even though I ran my holistic health business for many years, I was never very good at including pamper time for myself. I could, however, use my wonderful clients as a fine example. Many of my ladies were with me for over seven years. They made repeat appointments for a monthly treatment. That might have been a reflexology session, a back massage, or a meditation class. They found the time because they were 100 percent committed to their health and well-being. If, like me, you tend to forget to look after yourself on occasion, a simple bubble bath on a Sunday afternoon will work. Whatever you decide to do, make sure you add it to your calendar (or your weekly intention list).

Our goals will happen if we drive them forward, so staying motivated is important. However, it's also essential that we remember to have fun and live life to the full. Stressing ourselves out when we don't achieve a task or feel unmotivated for a day can only lead to negative feelings, and that's not what we want. If you don't manage to do something today, or this week, try again tomorrow, or next month.

DON'T SWEAT IT!

I HOPE you're finding the motivation you need as you read this book, and I genuinely want you to be feeling uplifted and inspired by the time you get to the end. However, we all have bad days. In fact, most of us have probably had a pretty crappy week or two, if not more, at some point in our lives. I wanted to include an entire section on the flip side to motivation, not so it undoes all the good work we've done so far but to show you that, even after a rubbish day or a life-changing bolt out of the blue, you can still pick it all up where you left off and move forward because those are the building blocks of motivating yourself to succeed.

Many of the self-help books that I read will power through to the end of whatever subject they are covering until you arrive at the light bulb moment, which is great. But there has been the odd occasion when I've been partway through an exercise and abandoned the book entirely because of a bad mood, an off day, or a lack of inspiration. I think it's important to accept the fact that "shit happens," and sometimes it's out of our control. Learning to deal with issues and then carrying on is a *huge* achievement, and if you've ever done this, pat yourself on the back. I wanted to share a personal story with you in the hope that it proves how strong we can be—how those inner passions, dreams, and goals never really disappear during dark times, but just sit out of reach until we're ready to get going again when the time is right. I wanted to share a story that says "don't sweat it!"

I started writing this sequel-that's-not-a-sequel almost immediately after *How I Changed My Life in a Year* was released, mainly because all the questions people were asking me were still fresh in my mind, but also because I didn't want to stop my regular writing routine. It was important to me that I stuck to my writing goals.

Thanks to taking part in that first NaNoWriMo contest, I had knuckled down to writing my young adult fantasy fiction and was able to write the trilogy over three years. As it happens, the fiction work became a lifesaver for me. A few years ago, I was finally diagnosed with severe depression and anxiety following the illness that wiped me out and forced me to close my holistic health business. On the surface, I was my usual bubbly self, but behind closed doors, I was a mess. I tried so many times to write this book, but every time I read my work back, I got frustrated. The "voice" wasn't the same—*my* voice wasn't the same.

Writing for the self-help/personal development genre is an honour, as you get to help hundreds of people who are on a unique journey. That could be a voyage of self-discovery or an excursion towards a better life, and then there are the women who, like me, survived abuse and are driving forward with rebuilding their broken lives. If I want to help these people, I have to be honest, and I have to be *authentic.*

How could I write about feeling motivated, being inspired to try new things, and setting goals when it took all my effort just to get out of bed each day? So, I threw the manuscript in the bin. Over thirty thousand words were shredded, and I climbed back under the duvet to sulk. I've battled like crazy ever since to get my mojo back. I've struggled with feelings of insecurity, fraud, and guilt that I attend events as a self-help author, yet once I'm back home, I crumble into a sobbing mess. I was desperate and scared, and nothing I did helped. So, for a time, I turned my back on everything I'd learned as a holistic health practitioner and disappeared into myself.

It took a long time, counselling, and the support of my family and a few incredibly reliable friends to start the slow journey back to being me again. At quite a few points, I never thought I'd feel normal again, and I certainly never thought I'd ever write nonfiction again, not unless it was a memoir about how bloody awful depression is.

After I'd sulked for a considerable number of months, I began to notice the old effective habits returning. I picked up my journal one evening and poured out everything I was feeling; it felt amazing, and I had the best night's sleep after doing it. I joined a gym and started to use the treadmill, walking at first until I was able to attempt a gentle jog. This might not sound like a huge deal, but when I was suffering the full brunt of my symptoms, I wasn't able to walk for five minutes without having to sit and rest. My mum used to leave me with all the mobility scooters and elderly shoppers who were parked on benches dotted around town, while she ran to grab the shopping. As it happens, I met some lovely old ladies and a few silver foxes on those outings!

I plugged my earphones in and relistened to my Headspace app, letting Andy Puddicombe's hypnotic voice calm and ground me. A friend of mine, Laura, qualified in Reiki healing, and I began going to her for regular sessions. Another therapist friend, Caroline, tried the EMMETT treatment on me with startling results. EMMETT is a popular technique used to assist in the relief of pain and discomfort. My journal was used night after night, I built up my stamina at the gym until I was jogging nonstop for twenty minutes, and I was smiling again.

It's ironic that after writing a book called *How I Changed My Life in a Year*, my entire life changed yet again in the space of a few months. I was bitten by a bug or a spider; we don't know the exact species of the vampire that caused so much damage, but my body began to react to the viral infection it left me with. I would lose the feeling in my arm and hand, I was utterly exhausted at the drop of a hat, and my legs vibrated so strongly I felt like I'd been plugged in and left on standby. There were so many different symptoms that I didn't know from one day to the next what I would be dealing with when I woke up. I could tick everything on the Lyme disease symptom checker, and yet every test returned as a negative. I guess it was inevitable that with the stress of this undiagnosed illness, the hospital visits, closing my much-loved business, running a home, and keeping the kids fed and watered, I would blow a fuse; the dark fog of depression descended very quickly and without remorse.

I called upon my cheerleading squad to help out. My parents (the baseline) were fabulous and rallied around to help in every way imaginable. My dad tried hard to help me find my nonfiction writing mojo by suggesting that I write a book called "How I Changed My Life Back Again!" We giggled at this, but I wished more than anything that I could do it. Instead of writing motivational paragraphs, I turned to my fantasy fiction, and this is where I remained for a long time.

I completed my young adult Guardians trilogy, sticking with that routine of writing something every day. Interestingly, it was my editor, Susan, who helped me understand how my depression was influencing my writing. The third book in my trilogy is quite dark: the main character hears voices and is tempted to the dark side. In short, it's exactly how I was feeling myself when I wrote it. Susan told me it was her favourite book of the series, and that struck a nerve with me. My "voice" hadn't gone; it had just changed to accommodate these new scenarios. I was still me, still a mum with bills to pay and a business to run; I just had to do things a lot slower and take a nap most afternoons.

With every day that passed, I noticed the subtle changes in my behaviour and thoughts, and I began to piece together all the parts of who I was and stick them back together. Using adult colouring books gave me time to sit quietly and contemplate. Meditation helped me to feel grounded and more in control of my body. Both of these things I had in my motivational toolbox. I've repeated the importance of self-care a few times in this book, but it was during this period that I valued the necessity of it more than ever. I have always told my clients that they can't fix others if they are broken, and here I was, broken almost beyond repair but trying to carry on as if I was the same person inside and out.

Just before I went for my first MRI scan, I held a vision board workshop for a group of employees at a local business. There were ten in the session, and the boards they created were varied and powerful. Before I did the workshop, I'd tried to make myself a board so that I could take it along as an example. In my head, I was still thinking about all the things I wanted to achieve and the nonfiction book I was trying to write. I looked for images of writers, books, upbeat affirmations, and anything else that represented that ideal. I cut, arranged, and stuck what I had collected on my board and then stopped. The board was only half-covered, and the images were muted colours of dark brown or black. There was a coffee cup, a pair of legs sticking out of a parked camper van, a lady relaxing in a bath, and three quotes. The first said, "life in the slow lane," the second said, "make time for what matters," and the third was one of my favourite quotes from Gandhi: "There is more to life than simply increasing its speed."

I stepped back and looked at the vision board I'd created, and everything fell into place for me. I needed to stop chasing goals and hold off on my dreams and desires, and I wanted to look after myself. There was no way I was going to achieve anything in the state that I was in. When I did the introduction to the workshop group and explained how their boards would reflect their true state of mind, they were dubious, until I showed them my pre-MRI board; this resonated with them, and they took to the course 100 percent and went home feeling inspired about their future. I left that workshop knowing exactly what I had to do.

I stripped everything back to basics. I neglected my motivational blog and only posted when I was having a good day. I threw that manuscript in the bin and informed my editor, Susan, who told me that I was incredibly brave, which spurred me on even more. I did so much self-care that I turned any guilt about being selfish entirely on its head, and in turn, I noticed that my daughter started running herself more bubble baths and indulging in a few duvet days. If I was teaching her that self-care was important, then I was winning on two fronts.

The household chore list got a revival as I struggled to cope with simple tasks, so the children stepped up and took on the responsibilities. They even started cooking a few meals. Granted, there were quite a few Birds Eye potato waffles consumed during that time, but I was overjoyed that they were taking on these tasks and helping out. The meal planners and online shopping techniques were lifesavers, and my cheerleading squad deserved Oscars for the support they provided. Life began to tick over once again until I was regularly writing in my journal and starting to plan for a future that only a few months before had looked bleak.

"Don't sweat it" became my new motto, and I lived by it as strictly as I could. As a fairly habitual control freak, I couldn't help but notice just how much I had changed. I didn't get wound up as much, I'd stopped getting the stress headaches that tightened like a vice around my scalp, the ridges on the inside of my mouth where I clench my teeth in my sleep had disappeared, my symptoms had become more manageable, and I could judge when a low day was coming or when an event would tire me out, so I could schedule a time-out afterwards.

My mojo came back a tiny bit at a time as I began to implement all the tools I've talked about in this book. I'd always known that they worked; I'd just never needed to use them in this way before. When I'd planned out the fifty-two challenges for my resolution challenge, I was in a totally different frame of mind, with a healthy body and a gregarious personality. I've become much more introverted over the past few years, but with it has come an inner wisdom and a much calmer persona. I knew the time was right to start writing this book the day I dug out my coloured pens and made a mind map of the chapter breakdown. It wasn't planned; I just woke up one day with a bubbling sensation in the pit of my stomach and a passion to write down the whirling thoughts. As a member of those empowering Facebook groups, I'd read so many wonderful posts about helping others to succeed, but I'd felt oddly detached from them, and then suddenly, like a flash of lightning, I knew that what I wanted to share could also help someone. I'd spent months commenting on other people's inspirational messages, and I'd even shared how lost I'd felt and received a landslide of supportive comments, but until that moment, I remained one step behind. Doing that mind map was a turning point for me, and I loved every moment of plotting what I wanted to say. That passion grew until I was scribbling down ideas in my notebook. It rose up when I was having coffee with friends, and they would comment on how I sounded like my old self. I know I'm a totally different person now; I know that along this journey I lost part of myself, but in among the darkness, I found a sliver of light, and I followed it.

I hope that by sharing this story it gives you a brief insight into how this book came to life—again—and how, no matter how bad your day gets, how unmotivated you might feel, or how drained of energy you get trying to push forward, it's going to be okay. You're not alone. Call on your cheerleading squad and use the techniques I've shared, or don't; leave it all for a while and come back when you feel ready, stronger, and wiser.

I'm a great believer in things happening for a reason. When I had to close my beloved holistic health business due to my illness, my clients and I, to some extent, saw it as a new beginning and a destiny that needed to be fulfilled. My wonderful ladies told me that I was meant to be writing and this illness was the universe giving me an almighty shove in the right direction. When I embraced this new freedom to write, I was plagued with an inability to put pen to paper. Now, I think that I had a different lesson to learn before I could move on. Maybe that's true, or maybe my only lesson for this life is to slow down, appreciate everything I have, and not sweat it.

There are several techniques that you can use if you find yourself feeling unmotivated, especially if you're in a similar situation. It's perfectly natural to be overwhelmed at certain points, and as we discussed earlier, our habits can see us resorting to the "I can't do this" mind-set too easily. You end up fighting an internal war, which leaves you feeling even worse and can have a detrimental effect on your health and well-being.

I've had more than my fair share of feeling sorry for myself, thinking the world is falling apart, and not being able to see anything worth celebrating. Bouncing back isn't always easy, but I felt it was important to include a few tips to show you that it *is* possible.

One of the things I noticed about my situation was how I seemed to be endlessly talking about my health problem, the fact I'd had to close my business, and the ongoing saga of daily symptoms. I was sick to death of hearing myself talk about it, but for a while after any huge shift or a change in life/situation, it's human nature to tell people. We've all done it, whether we're recounting the woes of our own situation or asking someone we haven't seen for a while how they are and getting the full story, in graphic detail. I ended up saying "I'm fine, thank you" because if I'd had to tell anyone about my symptoms or numerous hospital visits again, I'd have screamed.

Talking therapies such as CBT or professional counselling sessions are incredibly important for numerous situations, such as grief, abuse, and mental health issues, and I know they have benefited many of my friends and clients, but what I'm talking about is the continuous social chatter—the endless repetition of a hospital procedure or blow-by-blow account of daily symptoms. I stopped telling people how I felt and what was happening because, in the end, I was feeding off the worry, and it wasn't helping me to heal. If I was going to bounce back, I needed to turn my thoughts around and begin to think, act, and speak like a healthy person.

Using visualisation tools can help with this. Remember the vision board technique? This is an ideal way to visualise yourself as a healthy, determined individual. Revisit any boards you've already made and tweak them, or create a brand-new board centred on where you want to be in a few weeks/months/years.

Picture yourself in the future and notice that you're back in the frame of mind you were in before you felt unmotivated. You feel more determined than ever to succeed. You could even visualise yourself at the finish line.

More importantly, be kind to yourself. Shit happens. The pain will lessen, the fears will shift, change, or disappear, and the sun will rise again. My wonderful acupuncturist, Jo, often tells me that all the issues that I'm facing are bubbling up to the surface because I'm strong enough to cope with them at this time in my life. That's quite a reassuring way to look at it.

BE A WINNER

IF YOU purchased this book, then I'm guessing you are looking to make a few changes in your life—to feel optimistic, hopeful, and motivated to succeed in whatever challenge you have set for yourself.

I hope you've been able to pick up some valuable techniques that you can slot into your daily life with ease, reaping the benefits and experiencing that sense of achievement and pride that comes from completing something you've dreamed of having or set your heart on doing. When I receive messages from readers who feel inspired to set their own resolution challenges after following my blog or reading *How I Changed My Life in a Year*, they usually include a wide variety of topics from starting an Open University course, to blogging about a health issue and the road to recovery. They are all winners in my eyes, whether they complete the task or not.

Wanting to make a change or knowing that something isn't right, is the first step in becoming the person you want to be, and to be a winner, you must be ready to change your thoughts. We talked about vision boards earlier, and I shared one of my favourite quotes "Thoughts become things. If you see it in your mind, you will hold it in your hand" from Bob Proctor. Did you know that 70 percent of our daily thoughts are negative? Changing the way we think is paramount to achieving success. At the end of this book, I've included three lists.

One of them includes fifty-two affirmations—one for each week of the year. I have always found affirmations to be an excellent tool to turn my negative thoughts into positive ones.

Some affirmations are easier to say than others. I still, after all these years of self-work, find it hard to look at myself in the mirror and say "I love you." That's a huge lesson that I'm still working on, and I fully understand that this is down to issues I hold on to from my abusive marriage. Saying "I am a winner," however, is much easier for me to cope with, and to believe. By looking back over my goals, reviewing what I've done and achieved, and seeing the tiny messages mount up in my happiness jar, I know that I'm winning. Take a look at the list of affirmations and pick out the ones you like the most. Repeat them over and over to yourself, write them on a Post-it note and put them on your computer, fridge, or mirror. Use them to turn your negatives into positives and be a winner.

We all know that self-doubt and negative self-beliefs are unhelpful to our quest. People without any ambition, who are always living life in a glass-is-half-empty mind-set, tend to be unsuccessful in anything they do. If you believe in universal energy, you'll notice that someone who moans day after day about their lousy job, low pay, ill health, and miserable life will attract more of the same because this is what they are "putting out there." In basic terms, they are *asking* the universe for more of what they've got—thoughts become things.

To be a winner, we must change our thoughts, and more importantly, we must notice when we start the negative talk and correct ourselves—affirmations are great for that. In simple terms, an affirmation is the act of being in control of your thoughts. These short statements offer you support and encouragement and are incredibly powerful if repeated often.

If you don't like the idea of saying these things out loud, write them down and leave them dotted around your home or office, or pop one in your bag or purse, so you see it every time you open it. Writing down my achievements and adding them to my happiness jar is a technique that always drives me to focus on my goals going forward, especially if I reread them all on New Year's Eve. There's nothing stopping you from adding a few affirmations to your happiness jar, so they can jump out at you when you tip them out at the end of the year.

I was chatting with a friend recently and telling her about this particular exercise. She loved the idea; however, as she had experienced a particularly rough year with illness, loss, and redundancy, she didn't think she could find anything to add to her jar this year. I thought about this for a moment and realised that quite a few people might be in the same position. We have some years that are great, and other horrific ones where we wish we could start over or skip to the end. So, I suggested that she fill her jar with all the positive aspects of her *life* so far. I challenged her to make a "success" jar, filled with all the ballet competitions she'd won as a child, the swimming certificates, having her children, being successful at all the job interviews over the years, and anything else she could think of. Her mood changed immediately as she thought about this challenge differently. She became more positive about the exercise and even sent me a photograph of her jar later that week.

Being a winner is about learning everything we can throughout the journey and realising that we are strong, powerful, and successful women or men. It's perfectly understandable to lose your way occasionally; the last chapter showed you how that could be possible, but it also proved that most things are temporary, or if more permanent, how they can be adapted and worked around. Losing sight of what you want to achieve is going to happen at one time or another. It's a common side effect with women especially, as we still have a tendency to hold onto outdated beliefs about being the weaker sex. This can be overcome by grounding yourself and reclaiming your power. Giving my power away was something I did far too easily—sometimes without even realising it. It was such a simple action for friends/partners to suck me into negative relationships. Only after years of self-work can I now see the triggers and signs and rectify it before I willingly hand over my power again.

I read an article once about reclaiming your power or knowing how to bring yourself back to a winning formula. There were three questions you needed to ask yourself which, when given enough thought, would show you where you were at that moment in time.

- What is your deepest desire?
- What is your greatest regret?
- What will you do tomorrow to change the way you feel?

I found this to be quite an eye-opening exercise when I did it. My deepest desire was to be a writer and interestingly, my greatest regret was not having a partner to share my life with. For anyone who knows me well, this would come as a huge shock, as I've been incredibly vocal about never getting married again and loving my single-mum life. However, I wrote the first thing that popped into my head, and that was it. When it came to what I'd do the next day to change the way I felt, I decided to knuckle down with my writing projects and to work on my self-esteem and self-love, which would, in turn, open my heart up to the possibility of starting a relationship. For me, this was a gargantuan challenge, but it put me back in control of my life. Only I could make it happen by being the best me I could be.

Mixed in with my work on self-esteem I realised that all the years I'd spent procrastinating about doing what I'd always wanted to do had, in fact, fuelled my low self-respect. I'd spent so many years telling myself that I wanted to write a book, yet I'd never actually done anything to achieve this goal. Yes, I'd written a few flash fiction stories, had numerous letters and articles published, but the book or *books* remained a dream. I'm still pretty good at procrastinating; I blame social media and its lure to spend hours of your day on Twitter or pinning incredible images to your Pinterest boards. Of course, the *blame* lands firmly at my door because planning and organising myself would allow me the free time to enjoy the Facebook groups and Instagram posts. Procrastination is just another way of telling yourself "you're not worth it," and that's not what being motivated to achieve success is all about. My moments of weakness are much fewer than they were before I started my resolution challenge. Using the various techniques that I've shared in this book gave me back plenty of time where I could surf the net without any guilt, just as long as I had completed all my tasks.

Winners plan, they organise themselves, and they don't leave jobs half-finished. As I mentioned, writing was my main goal, but half-written books weren't going to make it onto the bookshelves in Waterstones. Ditching the procrastination and getting on with my action steps was the only way to do it. If you can relate to anything I'm saying, then here are a few tips to help you shake off that procrastination parasite:

Write down all the jobs you haven't finished yet. Include household chores like painting the bathroom and decluttering the cupboard under the stairs, as well as the main goals you've set for yourself. Work out which ones are the most important to you. Did you tell yourself that you would decorate the bathroom before Aunt Dotty came to visit in March? Perhaps your energy levels are feeling sluggish, and you know it's linked to the growing pile of shoes in that cupboard under the stairs. Jot a number next to the items on your list—number one being the top priority. Now think about that list again from a practical point of view. Do you *really* need to paint the bathroom, or will a good scrub be sufficient until you've got more time? Cross off all the jobs that can wait. Discard all the tasks that you've lost all interest in doing or finishing. Remember how I threw my first attempt at writing this book in the bin? I was on a spiral of procrastination when I tried to write anything, which left me feeling huge amounts of guilt, fear, and despair until I walked away.

My advice is to clear the jobs you can quickly and get all loose ends tied up and finished. Get rid of anything that doesn't excite you anymore. DO all the jobs that must be done (even if you really don't want to do them), assign a date, put it on your calendar, or in your diary as an appointment and then get them done. If Aunt Dotty is due next weekend, clear a day this weekend and get that bathroom looking fresh and fabulous. I guarantee you'll feel great once it's over, and you can even add it to your happiness/achievement jar.

Using these techniques is how you become a winner.

TRUST YOURSELF

One of the things I learned while doing my yearlong challenge was to trust myself—trust that I could handle this task and believe that I was strong enough to complete the projects. As I mentioned earlier, self-belief can be tough, but if you can find a way to trust in yourself, then winning will come much more easily to you.

Do you ever look at someone you know, or a celebrity you admire, and feel a gravitational pull towards them? You want to be near them, watch them on TV shows, or learn more about them. They are winners, and everyone loves a winner. Somewhere on their journey, this celebrity or friend/colleague has told themselves that they deserve to be or have the best. They then, in turn, attract oodles of excellent things into their life. They value themselves and can, therefore, lead a balanced life. Imagine this is you and your life; you are the one running a successful business, signing a three-book deal, getting married, losing weight, or succeeding in whatever goals you set for yourself.

I was told about a marvellous tip to help you believe in your own success by one of my mentors, and although it took some practice, I managed to visualise everything I needed, so I could experience the feeling of accomplishment. Try this and use the technique whenever you need to correct any negative thoughts. You can do it at any time of day or night, but I find that just before I go to sleep is the best time.

Imagine yourself sitting in a huge theatre. You are in the front row and feeling excited about seeing your favourite actor/actress/singer/entrepreneur/guru. They are giving a talk on how they achieved success and got to be where they are today. Every single seat in the theatre is sold out, and there is an eager vibe rippling through the audience. The lights dim, and the red velvet curtains sweep aside. The headline act steps forward to take their place in front of the microphone. You look up at the stage and see yourself standing there. The audience is clapping and cheering, and you are beaming back at them, happy to be standing in front of them and eager to share your story of success. Own it. Imagine picking up the microphone and addressing the packed theatre. Picture yourself walking across the stage confidently, chatting about your life and the goals you set for yourself. Share with them the lows and the moments you felt a little lost, and then feel the rush of adrenaline when you tell them how you turned those negatives to positives and achieved the ultimate goal. Hear them gasp, visualise them laughing along with your anecdotes, and see them clearly in your mind give a standing ovation when you've finished your speech. These people came to see *you*, they wanted to hear *you* speak, they spent hard-earned money to spend an hour or two in *your* orbit. Move over Oprah/Gabrielle Bernstein, ____________ (insert your name here) has arrived!

I adore this visualisation technique and found it incredibly useful when I was writing my first book. Instead of a theatre, I would sometimes imagine myself at a book signing, just like the one I attended for Sarah J. Maas, one of my favourite young adult authors. The queue of people waiting to meet her and have their book signed inspired me to imagine myself in a similar position. Adapt this exercise to suit your needs, but I urge you to have a go, as it's so powerful. It allows you to trust in yourself and believe that anything is possible.

A slightly different angle to this is learning to accept your uniqueness. If you've never quite felt like you fit in, picture yourself being authentic, quirky, or however you perceive your version of normal to be, and see the audience eagerly cheering you on. They wish they could be like *you*. They're sick of trying to blend in and just want to be genuine, just like *you*. This alternative visualisation came to me when I shared a meme on my young adult fiction Facebook page. It was a lovely image of one of my favourite actresses, Helena Bonham Carter, in one of her unique roles. She is wearing a corset dress with lashings of lace, and the wording says, "I wish it were socially acceptable to wear beautiful corset dresses or wizard cloaks every day." I loved the sentiment, and so I shared it on my page. That picture received tons of comments from my young adult followers, saying "Go girl, if you want to wear a wizard cloak, then wear it!" and "It's a free country, wear whatever you want," plus "I've got a purple corset dress and wear it all the time, love it!" It made me smile to know how unique my page followers were, especially when they were so young. They already knew how to embrace their uniqueness, and they were rocking it. They taught me a lot that day.

Shortly after that, I stopped analysing what I wore and welcomed my choice of wardrobe items. I'm a huge fan of black clothing, and it's always a shock to my friends and family if I turn up in a colourful outfit. I don't wear black because I hope it'll make me look two stone slimmer (if only); I wear it because I love it—I'm a bit like Wednesday Addams from *The Addams Family*. That's my uniqueness, and I'm happy to accept it. What's yours? What makes you, *you*? Trust in yourself, welcome the quirky parts, and attract good fortune. Being authentic will also bring the right kind of support, assistance, and results you are looking for.

GET A CONFIDENCE BOOST AND BANISH YOUR LIMITING BELIEFS

With self-belief, trust, and authenticity comes confidence. Setting yourself goals that are slightly out of your comfort zone can knock your confidence even more if you begin to doubt your abilities to succeed.

As a child and young teen I was incredibly confident, but as I got older, I began to allow too many limiting beliefs to take over and remove some of those extroverted tendencies. Living in a negatively controlling marriage for seven years stripped me of any remaining confidence that I had, reducing me to a weak, broken woman—an entirely different individual to who I'd been as a youngster.

If you're unsure of what a limiting belief is, it's a thought or belief that can seriously hold you back in life. They tend to work behind the scenes, lurking in the deep recesses of our brains, but they affect our actions in many ways. The majority of our limiting beliefs come from our childhood and are carried through our entire life span, tripping us up at various stages. They can include silly phrases your parents taught you before you could even walk, sayings that a teacher repeats to you throughout your school life, even damage done from words spoken in anger by a friend or spouse.

I can use my experiences to explain this better. I have a limiting belief about trust—I can't trust men. Why? Because I was betrayed by the one man who should have loved and supported me, my husband. This limiting belief has kept me from seeking a relationship and sent me running for the hills if anyone showed even the most remote interest in me. I've been single (alone) for thirteen years now. In other words, this limiting belief has affected a huge portion of my life. I continue to work on this in a variety of ways, including acupuncture, Reiki, and journaling. I also use CBT techniques to turn my thought patterns around and to recognise that not all men are untrustworthy. My wonderful dad, brother, sons, and other male family members and friends are far removed from this warped idea of men that my limiting belief has me believing.

Another example that you tend to see in adults is a belief that they are "not good enough." If you traced that limiting belief back to its source, odds are it was something a teacher used to say to you, something like "If you don't concentrate in class, you'll never amount to anything" or "Your results are poor; you need to try harder, or you'll fail." We've all heard these before, either being on the receiving end of it or occasionally the giver of such "advice." I've stopped myself so many times from saying to my kids "Buck up your ideas, or you'll not get very far." They are just throwaway comments, but the way we are wired means that they infiltrate our very being. I must just mention that teachers back in my day (the '70s and '80s) were very different from the teaching staff of today. Many teachers now understand the concept of limiting beliefs and use alternative language when they are talking to the children in their care. There are exceptions to this, however, and that's why it can be so important to understand what they are and how to spot them. In truth, they only really hold any weight because we decide they are true. Think about some of the phrases you've heard over and over:

- The old ball and chain = marriage is a prison.
- Time is money = you can only get money if you work every hour possible.
- Money doesn't grow on trees = money will never be easy to come by. You have limited funds. (OR, if you think about this phrase from a seasonal point of view, money isn't available all year long as leaves wither, die, and fall.)

Limiting beliefs are everywhere, and once you start to recognise them, you'll be able to break a few of your own and build your confidence. What about these?

- I'm not good with money.
- I'll never get the job I want.
- I always screw things up.
- I'm too old to change my career.
- I'm so dumb. (Often said in jest when you've done something silly, but think about it—what *exactly* are you telling yourself?)

From a resolutions/goal-setting point of view, you could prevent yourself from achieving all sorts of amazing things because of your limiting beliefs. What if your ultimate dream was to start your own business? Let's think back to the Baby Boo example in an earlier chapter. That could be the start of an amazing journey, working for yourself to fit around your family and earning decent money doing something you love. BUT, you could stop yourself by believing a simple phrase such as "I can't start my own business because I don't have the funds/time/space." When you utter that little word "because," you are telling your brain "there's a valid reason why I can't do this," and worse still, you *believe* it without even trying.

Take notice of the language you use when setting your goals. If you are brainstorming an idea and suddenly you feel an "I shouldn't even bother doing this because nobody will be interested in it" thought brewing, turn that thought on its head and instead ask yourself "How is this [idea] desirable/interesting/valid?"

When I began plotting out my book, I used this technique to highlight who I could help by writing these pages. Knowing that I could potentially support one young woman who was putting her life back together or hoping to reclaim her power and be the best she could be, was all I needed to invalidate that limiting belief that I wasn't good enough to write another book.

Using a page in your notebook to write down and capture your most frequent limiting beliefs can help you work on them one at a time to release them. Sometimes, it can be enough just to acknowledge them, taking away the power they have over you by simply knowing they exist.

It's quite easy to see other people's limiting beliefs because we are on the outside looking in, but to discover our own can be a tricky task. Don't give up; try to spot them by keeping an ear out for the "because" statements.

To rid yourself of limiting beliefs, you need to adopt a similar tactic to dealing with fear. Turning your viewpoint of a situation on its head often has the desired result. Imagine that your limiting belief is that you're too old to do anything new.

> *"I'm too old to change careers/go back to college/learn to use social media."*

I often feel like this about using social media and handling my marketing, and I'm only in my mid-forties. Technology moves so fast, and we have to be open to the changes, but if you were in your fifties, sixties, or older, then it might feel totally mind-blowing. Let's look at a scenario for a second.

Think about why you are holding on to the belief that you are too old to do something new. Perhaps you were told by your peers that older people are being overlooked in the workplace. How does that make you feel? I think I'd be despondent and grumpy. Now, spend some time thinking about who told you this vital statistic. Maybe it was fellow fifty-five-year-old Bill in accounting, who clings to a limiting belief that *he* is too old to learn a new skill. There's a strong possibility that it's just speculation based on his beliefs rather than a cold hard fact. So, if that's the case, *is* it true? You'll probably discover that there is no proof to back up Bill's announcement. That opens up a host of other thoughts for us to ponder.

If it isn't true, then there's a possibility that you're *not* too old to change careers/go back to college/learn to use social media. How does this change of thinking make you feel now? I'd be fairly excited about the prospect of retraining or getting a new job, wouldn't you? To reinforce your newfound belief and to squish that limiting one forever, the next time you see Bill, tell him about the Twitter eCourse you've just signed up for or the night class you're taking in anthropology. By accepting this new belief, you are telling yourself quite clearly that you're never too old to do something new. Go you!

I saw a fantastic video on Facebook recently about a seventy-five-year-old grandfather in Japan who started an Instagram account, so he could draw pictures and tell stories to his grandchildren who lived far away. He taught himself how to upload images and share them, and in the process, he "accidentally" gained over 180,000 Instagram followers who love his page.

If you search for them, there are stories of success from women and men of all ages and walks of life everywhere. Here are a few of my favourites:

- Louise Hay founded Hay House Publishing when she was in her fifties. She started this venture from her living room, and today, thirty years later, it's a prosperous corporation, selling millions of books and products across the world.
- J. K. Rowling's Harry Potter series was rejected by twelve publishers before Bloomsbury Publishing signed her. She went from being unemployed and on state benefits to becoming a multi-millionaire in five years.
- Alan Rickman didn't start his film career until he was forty-six years old when he was cast as the fabulous villain in *Die Hard*.

CONCLUSION

BEFORE I leave you to explore the remainder of this book, which includes a twelve-month productivity plan and four lists of fifty-two things to do: fifty-two uplifting quotes, fifty-two affirmations for success, and fifty-two power words, I wanted to sum up everything I've shared with you throughout this book.

Starting my blog back on 1 January 2013 was a life-changing experience for me. It opened up a host of opportunities, allowed me to meet so many new people, whether that was face-to-face or online, and prompted me to accomplish the only dream I'd had since I was eight years old: to write a book. That book was called *How I Changed My Life in a Year* because that's exactly what it did—it changed my life. Believe it or not, my life is nothing like it was before I published my book.

As I said before, you don't need to do anything as public as blogging, vlogging, starting a YouTube channel, or speaking at conferences. Stick to your comfort zones but do test yourself occasionally. Running a podcast might not be on your radar, but it might just be the challenge that lifts you out of a rut and drives you to plan an outstanding new future. I've learned so much since I began blogging, and I've met some amazing people. I now get to attend blogging awards and events; I've appeared in magazines, been a guest on popular websites, and presented workshops at women in business conferences, as well as been a guest speaker at various events and networking groups. None of this would have been possible if I hadn't dragged out my coloured pens one cold, miserable afternoon and done a mind map on how to complete my New Year's resolutions.

We've covered so many motivational tools in this book, and I hope I haven't blown your mind completely or overwhelmed you with choices. I think it's always best to find out how other people cope with goals and use the tools that resonate the most with your personal quest. Creating the right conditions to achieve success was the basis for this book. I wanted you to know how easy it is to shine. Learning these tools allows you to balance life, career, and self-care for the coming year, and beyond. So which personal development techniques and exercises do you think you'll use for your goal setting, planning, and action plans? I've added a tick list below as a reminder of everything we've talked about, so you can skip back to find the tools you like. I hope it helps:

☐ Closing-down ceremony

☐ To-do lists

☐ Creating SMART goals

☐ Mind maps

☐ Vision boards

☐ Assign rewards and celebrate achievements

☐ Wall planner, diary, calendar, apps

☐ Project planner

☐ 24-Hour daily clock planner

☐ Meal planners

☐ Batch cooking

☐ Online grocery shopping

☐ Household chore list

☐ Decluttering

☐ Self-care plan

☐ Body

☐ Mind

☐ Spirit

☐ Cheerleading squad

☐ Releasing fears

☐ Overcoming self-doubt

☐ De-stressing for success

☐ Case studies

☐ What is motivation?

☐ Changing habits

☐ Who motivates you?

☐ What motivates you?

☐ Shit happens!

☐ Be a winner

☐ Trust in yourself

☐ Getting confident

☐ Releasing limiting beliefs

☐ 52 Things to do

☐ 52 Uplifting quotes

☐ 52 Affirmations for success

☐ 52 Power words

☐ 52 Happy Weeks Challenge

Writing this book has been an emotional and inspirational journey for me. I started it, abandoned it, and then rediscovered it all over again. I hope you've enjoyed hearing about my story and can translate what I've said to fit your lifestyle. My blog is still going strong and has been rebranded from *Resolution Challenge* to the new name and logo of *Motivate Me!* I wanted it to evolve into a home for anyone who was looking for a bit of a boost to accomplish their dreams or a place to come if you needed guidance, support, or a giggle. I'd love you to join me there or interact with me on my Motivate Me Facebook page or on Twitter.

Blog: www.motivatemenow.co.uk

Facebook: www.facebook.com/MotivateMeBlog

Twitter: www.twitter.com/ShelleyWilson72

The best part of writing my blog and subsequent books has been the response from my readers. I receive so many messages of hope, inspiration, and thanks from women all over the world, and I am eternally grateful that they took the time to reach out and engage. Here are just a few of the messages that I've received over the past few years:

"Hi, I bought your book and read it over the last two evenings. I just wanted to say thank you; it's an inspirational book that feels so personal to me, as so many of your experiences are similar to mine. You have made me re-evaluate how I deal with challenges and motivated me to kick-start my dreams! Thank you for writing such an honest, real book." — Mala Franklin

"Hi, I just wanted to say a huge thank you for your book 'How I Changed My Life in a Year.' I've read it in two days flat and have enjoyed every second of it—so much of the book I could personally identify with and although I've been through the mill and the upshot now is that I'm in a wheelchair, I'm doing a degree in English lit and creative writing, and your book has helped me rationalise a lot of my fears. Thank you again." — Caz Potterton

"I have just read your book and just wanted to say how inspiring it is, and I have decided to follow in your footsteps and take on my own challenge! Thank you for writing this book." — Laurena Cornock

"Hello! I'm just dropping you a line to say how much I enjoyed your book. I really want to write, but stuff always seems to get in the way; I did start blogging, but again I just didn't have any structure in place, and it was all over the shop! I felt I failed and then gave up—I am a silly girl. Having been far too guilty of taking on too much, which results in me running about like a headless chicken for other people, I plan to reclaim myself! Thanks again, I have plans afoot to make things happen—finally!"
— Louise Wood

"Hi Shelley, I was inspired by your blog and your story. After much researching and thinking, I finally got around to setting up my blog. I would just like to say, thank you and keep up the good

work. It's amazing how other people's optimism can be so encouraging. I'm still exploring the world of blogging, but it's exciting." — Gloria McBreen

"I wanted you to know that I have just finished your book and found it inspiring. I have recently been wanting to change my path and my whole outlook on life. As a survivor of childhood sexual abuse, it has taken me a very long time to find my own self-worth (I'm forty now), but through my children, my husband, and counselling, I am stronger and better than that. I guess what I'm trying to get at is that your book has inspired me to reach higher and take my next step...so thank you for that." — Anna

"You are a true inspiration! I am also a single mum of three and also escaped an abusive relationship seven years ago (from the father of my two eldest children). I work every day and find very little time for myself. I found a review of your book and ordered it. I got home from work today to find that your book had been delivered. I read it all the way through in one night! Bloody brilliant! Thank you so much and well done you! I have to add, this is the first book I have read and finished in two years, all in one evening! I have already told all my friends to get a copy and sung your praises. Brilliant work." — Sara Buckett

"Your book is amazing and so are you! Massive congratulations on your success at life! I have just finished your book and loved every page from start to finish! Your book was truly wonderful to read, and I will most definitely recommend it to those who wish to live again and just simply be happy and healthy. I am a young mother aged twenty-two with two girls. I also left a toxic relationship! For this past year, I have been on a personal development journey, and it's the best breath of fresh air anyone can

breathe in! I could relate so much to your book and the ventures you embarked on. You are an inspiration. I know how hard our journey is as mothers and women! Well done." — Amy Taylor

YOUR TWELVE-MONTH PRODUCTIVITY PLAN

MY HOURS of brainstorming and creativity with a large sheet of paper and a set of coloured pens allowed me to create a twelve-month plan that would become the basis for my blog. Getting it down on paper was the first step to visualising the reality of what I hoped to achieve. Seeing the breakdown in twelve easy sections took away any anxiety I had before starting my resolution challenge.

As this was such a great exercise for me, I've added a quick productivity plan for you to fill in (if you're reading this as a paperback), or you can jot down your answers in a notebook. Feel free to use this if you still need a little bit of guidance, but if you feel motivated to get going on your own, then go for it!

MONTH ONE

Brainstorm your ideas and think about the goals you wish to achieve over the next few months.

____

____

TIP: don't forget to assign yourself a power word to keep you focused—there are fifty-two examples in the next chapter if you need some help. What's your power word of the year going to be?

MONTH TWO

Make a plan. Use the ideas from your brainstorming sessions to work out what you want to work on every week/month, and remember to break them down into manageable chunks.

MONTH THREE

Organise a meal planner for the next few weeks and order your shopping online. Try it out and see how much time you save yourself. Spend one day doing a batch cook, so your freezer is full of yummy dinners, leaving you with plenty of time to concentrate on your goals.

MONTH FOUR

Who's on your cheerleading squad? Seek the support of the people you can rely on to keep you focused on your goals and deadlines.

MONTH FIVE

Be proactive! Talking about your dreams doesn't make them happen. What action steps are you going to take this month to move forward with your goals?

MONTH SIX

Have you been taking care of your own needs? What self-care plan have you put in place to ensure that your health and well-being are nourished throughout the year?

MONTH SEVEN

Review it! Look back at the goals you set at the start of your twelve months. Are they going to plan? Are you ticking off the tasks on your to-do list? Do you need to make any changes so that the rest of the year is as successful?

MONTH EIGHT

Declutter. Take a look around and see if you've built up any clutter over the past few months. Not just physical "stuff" but also emotional clutter. Spend half an hour, or even a full day, sorting out a few spaces.

MONTH NINE

Write down those limiting beliefs that have been holding you back, and spend ten minutes rewording them and creating a new belief system built on success.

MONTH TEN

As you approach the end of your year, start to brainstorm a few ideas for the next set of goals you want to work on. These might be a continuation of what you're already working on or entirely new ideas. Begin the process now, and you'll be fully prepared when the time comes to start a new twelve-month plan.

MONTH ELEVEN

Reflect on what you've achieved so far. Was it everything you hoped it would be? Did you do everything you wanted to do? If not, why not? Are there any lessons you learned that will help you to succeed in the future?

MONTH TWELVE

Time to celebrate! Jot down the rewards that you are working towards. Are they physical treats like a new gym bag, face cream, notebook, or dress/shirt, or are they more practical like launching a workshop, releasing a debut novel, or starting that business? Celebrating your successes is the fun part, so think big!

52 WEEKS IN A YEAR: USE THEM WISELY

52 THINGS TO DO

I HAVE always been fascinated by the mind and how our thoughts shape what we do with our lives. Weight loss, for me, seemed to involve overthinking things—my lack of willpower and the inability to stop thinking about food, in particular.

To help lose weight, I had to rethink everything and start to live the life of a slim person. Do you notice that slim people *never* think about food? I began to do something different and pushed myself to try a new experience. It helped. I was able to start living my life without the constant overthinking patterns and poor food habits.

Changing habits isn't only beneficial for weight loss. I have used new experiences to push myself out of a rut on more than a few occasions. Procrastination is a favourite pastime of mine, and if I don't get that drive, then I can drown in organisational skills without ever accomplishing anything. Sound familiar? How many times have you promised yourself that you will do X or Y but seemed to find a hundred ways to avoid doing it?

I wanted to compile a list of things that I hope you will try as part of your motivational journey. I've done some, but not all, of this list. It includes the types of activities that will push you out of your comfort zone and make you do something different—one for each week of the year. Feel free to add your own ideas in your notebook and record every detail of the activities you choose to have a go at.

1. Look up your family tree.
2. Go to an outdoor music festival.
3. Learn how to change a tyre.
4. Donate blood.
5. Have your portrait painted.
6. Make a birthday cake.
7. Adopt an endangered animal.
8. Learn to ski/swim/snorkel.
9. Write a handwritten note to someone you haven't seen for a while and post it to them.
10. Learn sign language.
11. Forgive someone.
12. Drive/walk to work/college using a different route.
13. Volunteer for a charity event.
14. Eat fish-and-chips by the sea.
15. Sleep under the stars.
16. Learn to say "I love you" in a foreign language and use it on your family/friends.
17. Wish a stranger a lovely day.
18. Keep a diary.
19. Say "no" more.

20. Have a major declutter.
21. Make homemade bread.
22. Go out without your makeup on.
23. Watch a sunset or a sunrise (or both).
24. Sign up for a local community class.
25. Start or join a book club.
26. Make yourself a "motivate me" playlist.
27. Buy a diary/planner/calendar and use it.
28. Get a library card.
29. Go to the theatre or cinema by yourself.
30. Drink more water.
31. Pack a picnic and eat lunch outside in the park, by a lake or in the garden.
32. Swap the car for a bike for the day.
33. Take a guided tour of your local town or city.
34. Jump into the sea.
35. Fundraise for a local charity.
36. Take an art class.
37. Go out for ice cream (even if it's winter).
38. Make candles and give them as a gift.
39. Go tobogganing.
40. Make a list of everything you've done that you're proud of—celebrate your accomplishments
41. Turn your mobile phone off for a full day.
42. Write a thank you letter to your mum.
43. Send Valentine's cards to all your friends.

44. Reread your favourite childhood book.
45. Remove one unhealthy thing from your life (e.g. crisps, fizzy drinks).
46. Write a list of reasons why you're happy to be alive.
47. Make something crafty.
48. Book an alternative therapy—if you usually have a pedicure, try reflexology. If you always have a massage, opt for Reiki.
49. Have a film night and choose films that you wouldn't normally watch.
50. Call someone you haven't spoken to in a while.
51. Write down your life plan—just a guide of all the things you'd like to do—and tick them off as you do them.
52. Learn ten sentences in a new language.

52 UPLIFTING QUOTES

There is something wonderful about reading an uplifting quote, a mantra, or an amusing saying and finding that it resonates with your present situation. My office wall is covered in little signs, Post-it notes and scribbled-on scraps of paper—all with quotes that mean so much to me. They make me smile and can boost my confidence when I need it.

In this section, I have included fifty-two quotes, one for each week of the year, to give you a lift when you need it. I find that writing down your favourite saying and putting the piece of paper on your wall, fridge, or even in your purse can be very comforting. Read over the list and choose the ones that resonate with you the most. Say them out loud, shout them when you need to release any tension, or flick back to this page when you want to find the perfect words to match your week.

1. "Problems are not stop signs, they are guidelines." Robert H. Schuller
2. "Discouragement and failure are two of the surest stepping stones to success." Dale Carnegie
3. "Once you choose hope, anything's possible." Christopher Reeve
4. "The best way to predict the future is to create it." Abraham Lincoln
5. "If I persist long enough I will win." Og Mandino
6. "In the middle of difficulty lies opportunity." Albert Einstein
7. "Light tomorrow with today." Elizabeth Barrett Browning
8. "Do not let what you cannot do interfere with what you can do." John Wooden
9. "If there is no struggle, there is no progress." Frederick Douglass
10. "Rise above the storm and you will find the sunshine." Mario Fernandez
11. "The best is yet to be." Robert Browning
12. "Believe you can and you're halfway there." Theodore Roosevelt
13. "Life is 10 percent what happens to you and 90 percent how you react to it." Charles R. Swindoll
14. "It always seems impossible until it's done." Nelson Mandela

15. "Never give up, for that is just the place and time that the tide will turn." Harriet Beecher Stowe
16. "The best way to cheer yourself up is to try to cheer somebody else up." Mark Twain
17. "Count your age by friends, not years. Count your life by smiles, not tears." John Lennon
18. "I've been absolutely terrified every moment of my life—and I've never let it keep me from doing a single thing I wanted to." Georgia O'Keeffe
19. "Twenty years from now you will be more disappointed by the things that you didn't do than by the ones you did do. So throw off the bowlines. Sail away from the safe harbour. Catch the trade winds in your sails. Explore. Dream. Discover." Mark Twain
20. "Happiness is not something ready-made. It comes from your own actions." Dalai Lama
21. "Do not go where the path may lead; go instead where there is no path and leave a trail." Ralph Waldo Emerson
22. "There is more to life than simply increasing its speed." Mahatma Gandhi
23. "It's never too late—never too late to start over, never too late to be happy." Jane Fonda
24. "Why not just live in the moment, especially if it has a good beat?" Goldie Hawn
25. "This life is not for complaint, but for satisfaction." Henry David Thoreau
26. "Opportunities don't often come along. So, when they do, you have to grab them." Audrey Hepburn
27. "My sun sets to rise again." Robert Browning

28. "Shoot for the moon. Even if you miss, you'll land among the stars." Les Brown
29. "Laugh as if it's funny, embrace as if it's love, and smile anyway." Richelle E. Goodrich
30. "Plunge boldly into the thick of life, and seize it where you will, it is always interesting." Johann Wolfgang von Goethe
31. "One setback is one setback—it is not the end of the world." Jillian Michaels
32. "Achieving a goal is nothing. The getting there is everything." Jules Michelet
33. "Experience is the name everyone gives to their mistakes." Oscar Wilde
34. "Clinging to the past is the problem. Embracing change is the answer." Gloria Steinem
35. "If you don't risk anything, you risk even more." Erica Jong
36. "Everybody has talent, it's just a matter of moving around until you've discovered what it is." George Lucas
37. "It's our choices, Harry, that show what we truly are, far more than our abilities." Albus Dumbledore
38. "Your vision will become clear only when you can look into your own heart. Who looks outside, dreams; who looks inside, awakes." Carl Jung
39. "Learn to get in touch with the silence within yourself, and know that everything in this life has purpose. There are no mistakes, no coincidences. All events are blessings given to us to learn from." Elisabeth Kubler-Ross

40. "The best thing about the future is that it comes one day at a time." Abraham Lincoln
41. "Freedom lies in being bold." Robert Frost
42. "The real voyage of discovery consists not in seeking new landscapes, but in having new eyes." Marcel Proust
43. "The emotions are an incredible gift that we have to let us know what we're thinking." Bob Doyle
44. "If you see it in your mind, you will hold it in your hand." Bob Proctor
45. "The spiritual substance from which comes all visible wealth is never depleted. It is right with you all the time and responds to your faith in it and your demands on it." Charles Fillmore
46. "Nothing is impossible, the word itself says 'I'm possible.'" Audrey Hepburn
47. "I don't go by the rule book. I lead by the heart, not the head." Princess Diana
48. "Find something you are passionate about and keep tremendously interested in it." Julia Child
49. "If you are always trying to be normal, you will never know how amazing you can be." Maya Angelou
50. "The critical ingredient is getting off your butt and doing something. It's as simple as that. A lot of people have ideas, but there are few who decide to do something about them now. Not tomorrow. Not next week. But today. The true entrepreneur is a doer, not a dreamer." Nolan Bushnell
51. "Smile! It increases your face value." Truvy, *Steel Magnolias*

52. "She stood in the storm, and when the wind did not blow her way, she adjusted her sails." Elizabeth Edwards

52 AFFIRMATIONS FOR SUCCESS

An affirmation is a simple action of affirming something. It can be a word or a phrase used to offer support or encouragement, for ourselves or others. I use them on a daily basis, and they have become so ingrained in my life now. From repeating the word "release" over and over when I want to let go of a bad memory or disagreement, to telling myself "I am healthy and happy in my own skin," which I normally repeat around the summer months for swimsuit season.

I often suggest specific affirmations to clients who are struggling with a particular issue. I ask them to repeat a word or a phrase over and over, in their head, or out loud. Affirmations are powerful.

In the list below, I've added fifty-two of my favourite affirmations. You can pick one to use for each week of the year or choose a couple that resonate with your life/emotions and use them repeatedly. It works best if you say them in the morning and then again at night. Put yourself in a positive frame of mind as you use these affirmations. Picture the words as if they are a true representation of your life. For example, "I attract all the money I need to fulfil my greatest desires." Repeated morning and night with passion, energy, and a positive vibe, they will help you to feel rich, and in true cosmic ordering style, this will, in turn, attract all the money that you need to fulfil your greatest desires. *Dream it. Live it. Become it.*

1. I attract all the money I need to fulfil my greatest desires.
2. I am happy with myself for being healthy and energetic.
3. I find happiness in the smallest things.
4. I am the luckiest person I know.

5. I am proud of my body.
6. I am pleased with myself for living a well-balanced lifestyle.
7. I am secure in my ability to talk to other people.
8. I am grounded, protected, and safe for the day/week ahead.
9. I am free of blood pressure problems (or insert another ailment) and free of all life-threatening diseases.
10. I am full of energy, and my mind is calm and peaceful.
11. I visualise, plan, and action my ideas.
12. I embrace change and turn it to my advantage.
13. I avoid junk food.
14. I am disciplined with my spending.
15. I love myself, and I am happy and healthy.
16. I always attract the resources to do whatever needs to be done.
17. Money comes easily, frequently, and abundantly into my life.
18. I have a wonderful and fulfilling relationship with my husband/wife/children.
19. I am a leader who inspires others to do great things.
20. I am a great listener.
21. I have a passion for everything I do in life.
22. I can always strive for better.
23. Great opportunities come my way, and I take advantage of this.
24. I am a problem solver.

25. I am always in the right place at the right time.
26. I treat others the way I want to be treated.
27. I let go and release everything that is not beneficial to me.
28. I am purpose driven, and all the right doors open for me.
29. Every day is full of hope, health, and happiness.
30. I am a highly influential person.
31. All my bills are paid in full, and I have money to spare.
32. I am confident and assertive.
33. Every day I become more prosperous.
34. Good things happen to me every day.
35. I give generously to myself and others.
36. I attract success easily.
37. I am earning a big income doing what makes me happy.
38. The more love I give, the more love I receive.
39. I see myself living a life of abundance and wealth.
40. I am gentle and kind to myself, knowing that I am doing the best I can.
41. I attract loving people into my life.
42. I believe that I can achieve anything I want to.
43. What I was yesterday no longer exists. What I am today is what matters.
44. I am an interesting human being.
45. I am a success magnet.
46. I am a strong woman/man.
47. I accept my age with joy and pride.
48. I grow more beautiful and less fussy as I grow older.

49. I lovingly take care of my body.
50. I like my thighs, stomach, and bum, and take care of them with exercise.
51. I am a money magnet.
52. Age is a state of mind, and mine is in one happy state.

52 POWER WORDS

I mentioned in the first section of this book the importance of having a power word to set your intention for a new year/month/project. Here are some of the words I have used over the years as well as a few suggestions that might resonate with you:

1. Strength
2. Happiness
3. Kindness
4. Loyalty
5. Love
6. Beauty
7. Childhood
8. Experiences
9. Focus
10. Grateful
11. Imagination
12. Joy
13. Laughter
14. Motivation
15. Neighbourhood
16. Connected

17. Divine
18. Open
19. Power
20. Quiet
21. Peace
22. Thankful
23. Universal energy
24. Vision
25. Me
26. Silliness
27. Health
28. Enjoyment
29. Remarkable
30. Delicious
31. Business
32. Goals
33. Pioneering
34. Willpower
35. Attractive
36. Fortune
37. Training
38. Simplified
39. Professional
40. Rewards
41. Revolutionary
42. Authentic

43. Revisited
44. Confident
45. Awesome
46. Creativity
47. Support
48. Progress
49. Teamwork
50. Family
51. Delegate
52. Spiritual

52 HAPPY WEEKS CHALLENGE

A few years ago, I took part in the 100 Happy Days Challenge on my blog. The link to that blog post is still one of the most viewed after four years of blogging. It was a challenge that brought out the best in everyone who took part. The idea was a simple one—for one hundred days you had to post a picture on your social media platform (that could be Facebook, Twitter, Tumblr or Instagram) of something that made you happy that day. I posted a photograph of a new mug that one of my clients bought me; then I posted a selfie with my daughter; another day I put an image of the sun shining—you get the idea. It was not only great fun to take part and interact in the trending hashtag #100HappyDays, but it also made me more aware of my surroundings and what I did every day. I actively searched for happiness, and by doing this exercise, I realised how many wonderful things I'd been missing out on. There's a fabulous quote that, for me, sums up the 100 Happy Days challenge:

"Take time to smell the roses,

Take time to enjoy the view,

And as you stop to enjoy the beauty,

Take time to reflect on love."

~ Laura D. Field. ~

So, here is my challenge to you. Find your "happiness" for each week of the year. I'm not asking you to commit to one hundred days; I'm asking you to find one thing that makes you happy each week for the next year. If you're struggling to find things, I've included my happiness list below as a guide—now, write your own, and if you feel inspired to share your 52 Happy Weeks Challenge images, post them on your Facebook page or Instagram feed.

1. My three amazing children
2. My wonderfully supportive parents
3. Shopping for new books
4. Harry Potter!
5. The smell of freshly cut grass
6. My beautiful black cat, Luna
7. Enjoying coffee with friends
8. Scented candles
9. A morning at the gym
10. Batch cooking
11. *Buffy the Vampire Slayer* DVD marathon on a rainy day
12. Seeing my nephew
13. Mum and daughter days
14. New stationery

15. Watching vampire films
16. Reading
17. Blogging
18. Writing
19. Eating chocolate
20. Johnny Depp!
21. Binge-watching Netflix shows
22. Tigers
23. My computer
24. Watching the snow fall and not having to go anywhere
25. Hot chocolate with whipped cream and marshmallows
26. Looking at the stars
27. Christmas markets
28. Zentangling (a form of doodling)
29. Halloween
30. Christmas
31. Lazy summer Sundays
32. Banana cake
33. Gazing at the full moon through my telescope
34. Christmas Eve anticipation
35. Chamomile tea
36. Adult colouring books
37. A large latte from Costa
38. Dancing to music in my kitchen
39. Decluttering
40. Meditating

41. Making a vision board on New Year's Eve
42. Going to the cinema
43. Pepperoni pizza
44. Being by the sea
45. A share bag of Maltesers to myself!
46. Meeting lovely people
47. Travelling
48. Reflexology
49. Talking about books
50. Going to the theatre
51. A good night's sleep
52. Kicking autumn leaves

A FINAL WORD OF THANKS

I HOPE you've gained some inspiration from this book and are feeling upbeat and excited about getting stuck into whatever challenge you feel ready to tackle. As always, I would love to hear your feedback, so please don't hesitate to get in touch with me, either via my blog or social media.

Your messages of encouragement and support are hugely appreciated, as too are your reviews, so if you could spare a few moments to share your thoughts, I would be eternally grateful. Who knows, your message might be featured in my next book!

Some of the topics I've covered here are daily factors in people's lives, such as depression, cancer, epilepsy, and abuse. If you need further information about any of the organisations who help support these issues, then the following links may be useful.

Epilepsy Research UK: www.epilepsyresearch.org.uk
Women's Aid: www.womensaid.org.uk
Mesothelioma Cancer: www.mesothelioma.com
Depression and Anxiety: www.mind.org.uk

All that's left for me to say is a massive thank-you from the bottom of my heart. Thank you for buying this book, for joining me on this journey, and for trusting me to be a part of yours. When I write, it's with the aim of being as honest, open, and helpful as I can be. Hopefully, you've found something within these pages that ticks all of those boxes.

Good luck to you as you embark on the next adventure in your life, whatever that may be. You are unique, loved, appreciated, and full of strength, power, and determination—never forget that!

ACKNOWLEDGMENTS

In no particular order, I'd like to thank:

Lee, Jamie, and Ella, your endless encouragement has been my lifeline. Your unwavering belief that I would succeed kept me writing. I love you so much xxx

My incredible parents who have celebrated every high point and been there to dust me down when I hit a low point. You encouraged me at every stage and supported me through life. I love you both and continue to be inspired by your actions xx

My family and friends. You have listened to my stories and given me feedback; you became the voice of encouragement when I needed it. You are my inspiration x

Thank you to Sooz, for your patience, professionalism, and dedication to helping me bring this book to life.

The list would not be complete without a shout-out for Peter Jones from Soundhaven.com. You kept me sane, kept me writing, and kept me laughing. Thank you from the bottom of my heart.

Finally, thanks to you, the reader, for picking up this. I hope it lived up to your expectations.

Thank you all.

ABOUT THE AUTHOR

Shelley Wilson divides her writing time between motivational non-fiction and fantasy/horror for young adults. She also writes a multi-award winning motivational personal development blog and has been named one of the Top 10 UK Personal Development Blogs.

Shelley was born in Leeds, West Yorkshire but raised in Solihull, West Midlands, UK, where she lives with her three teenagers.

www.shelleywilsonauthor.co.uk
www.facebook.com/MotivateMeBlog
www.twitter.com/ShelleyWilson72
www.instagram.com/authorslwilson
www.bhcpress.com

Printed in July 2019
by Rotomail Italia S.p.A., Vignate (MI) - Italy